Tying the Knot

To: Ms. Davis
May God continue
to bless you

Michele
Keep Hopping
Thornton

THE WOMEN'S FAITH AND BUSINESS MINISTRY

The Women's Faith and Business Ministry serves as a much-needed tie between business and ministry to equip women, and the men who serve with them, to operate in kingdom principles. We create a pathway to share wisdom and encouragement through skill-based trainings, networking, social media, seminars, and our annual conference.

Connect with Debora D. Taylor for your next event:
Website: *www.DeboraDTaylor.com*
Facebook: *Facebook.com/groups/WomensFaithandBusiness/*
Email: *DeboraDTaylor@DeboraDTaylor.com*
Phone: 888.584.9058

Taylor-Made International
P.O. Box 1554
Collierville, TN 38027

Available Services
   Motivational Speaking and Teaching
   Business Coaching
   Leadership Training
   Executive and Group Travel Consulting
   Spiritual / Life Coaching

Tying the Knot

BETWEEN MINISTRY AND THE MARKETPLACE

The Women's Faith and Business Series
Volume 1

DEBORA D. TAYLOR, FOUNDER

Cover Design and Layout:
Brennan Hill * Bhill Arts & Graphics * *BHillArts@gmail.com*

Interior Design and Layout:
Dell Self * Speak Through Me Publishing * *www.STMPub.net*

Disclaimer:
The content provided within this book is for general informational purposes only. The methods described within this book are the authors' personal thoughts. They are not intended to be a definitive set of instructions for your life. You are responsible for any use of this material.

DEDICATION

With gratitude, I dedicate this book to the co-authors for their support in compiling our first anthology: The Women's Faith and Business Series, Volume 1: *Tying the Knot Between Ministry and the Marketplace*. Every idea in this book bears the author's fingerprint—an original identity the Lord gave each of them.

"You are the light that shines for the world to see."
—Matthew 5:14 ERV

CONTENTS

FOREWORD

Upon meeting Debora Taylor, we immediately realized we had discovered a precious jewel. She is a woman who has found a way to balance family, the pastorate, evangelism, and marketplace ministry unlike few we have had the opportunity of meeting. As a woman of God, Debora not only produces results, but has the ability to turn others into producers. She has knowledge and wisdom, and is willing to share her information with others.

After their retirement and transition from the pastorate, Debora, and her husband, Guy Taylor, met our bishop in Milwaukee, Wisconsin, informing him of their intentions to meet and connect with us in Memphis, Tennessee. Soon afterwards, along with a few conversations over lunch, they visited our church. As our church visions and passions for community mirrored one another, we were convinced it was the will of God for us to connect.

God has entrusted Debora to have numerous high-level relationships in the religious community and in the business and political arenas as well. She has done a tremendous job at mending all these mountains of influence in her efforts at advancing the kingdom of God in a mighty way. Debora's desire to see Christian women become successful in the marketplace is evident as she galvanizes them through her Women's Faith and Business Ministry forums.

Debora is such an involved people-person. She has an incredible insight that the body of Christ desperately needs. Her proficiency in spearheading and pursuing the fatherhood initiative on a national level speaks to her ability to infiltrate territories usually dominated by men. She teamed up with our church and us as we re-launched The Husband Institute,

Inc., a non-profit organization, 501(c)(3), for mentoring boys in the Memphis area.

In her own life she is multi-talented, family-oriented, and business-diverse. Her smile and her ability to encourage and support the endeavors of others are undeniable. Debora's expertise in connecting and partnering people with others and with business resources is invaluable.

As you read this book, you'll be enlightened, you'll feel the love of God, and you'll gain wisdom from Debora and her friends which will launch you in the direction of your visions, dreams, and goals. Enjoy!

Apostle Ricky and Pastor Sheila Floyd
The Pursuit of God Transformation Center
Memphis, Tennessee

ACKNOWLEDGMENTS

I want to say thank you to my husband, Guy, for his love, support, and patience. My daughter, Nyshi, for inspiring and encouraging me to go forth with this book project for women. I love you more than words can express.

To my book project manager, Dell Self (Speak Through Me Publishing), for her tireless collection of data organization and implementation that gave birth to this publication.

Thank you to John Keller for allowing God to work through you in such a quiet way. Many have been blessed because of your obedience in listening to God.

Thank you Brennan Hill (Bhill Arts & Graphics) for jumping in and saving the day with an awesome book cover design.

Finally, to my priceless son, Dominique Lamar, and to my two granddaughters, My'Asha and Gracelyn, indeed you are my generational legacy.

An Interview with the Founder

As the founder of the Women's Faith and Business Ministry, Debora Taylor has a wealth of insight to share with women across the country. We thought it best to hear her heart in her own words by way of an interview. Debora has an inspiring story wrapped in depth and insight.

Question:
What led to the creation of the Women's Faith and Business Ministry? What's the story behind the ministry?

Debora:

After twenty-nine years of being an employee, I found myself propelled into a transformational season in my life. I began to mull over some tough questions, personally and professionally. I asked myself, "Is it too late to make a career change from employee to entrepreneur when you are over fifty?" "Does God really have a purpose for me in this of season of my life?" "Do I really want to work for another organization or company?" "What will it take to be successful in reinventing myself as an entrepreneur?" "What are the rules for starting my own business?"

There were a number of things I didn't know, but there were at least a few things I did know. I knew leadership success when I saw it. I knew how to nurture connections, networks, and collaborations. I knew how to build partnerships. I knew how to play well with others. I was convinced there was greatness inside of me that connected to the success I desired—there had to be.

Just as there are four seasons—winter, spring, summer, and fall, each with its own challenges, yet each season fulfills its own purpose. Suddenly, I realized this season of my life was temporary. A new season was fast approaching; it could only emerge as spring or summer.

After seeking the Lord through prayer, fasting, and meditation, I understood my purpose was to make a difference in the lives of people, especially women. This part would not change; but the method of execution would change. Sometimes we let our busyness in our daily activities, noise in our heads, fear in our hearts—even tainted motives, drive out our sense of purpose. Our Creator has given us, not just a job, the church, or people. God has given us vision and purpose. Listen, if you do not walk in your purpose you become another pretty face lost in the crowd. Whether as a minister, speaker, author, entrepreneur, consultant, teacher, trainer, business owner, coach, mentor, mother, grandmother, or wife; I continue to be a woman called by God and driven to make a difference.

As I stood on the shoulders of my faith with special determination, striving, and surviving in the midst of the worst transition in my life, I received some of my greatest awards and honors, including the National Presidential Community Service Award given to me by President Barack Obama. I served within the National Practitioners Leadership Institute, as an inaugural member, mentor, and advisor to many of the federal, regional, state, and local non-profit and for profit programs. In June 2013, the chairwoman of the Board (at my employment) gave me the highest honor an employee could receive from that agency. Yes, that same agency that was about to lay me off, honored me with the "Chairperson Award of Excellence." What's so amazing is that in the fifty-year history of that agency, only one other person has received this award. Guess what? She was a woman too! My name will be forever hanging inside the boardroom of the organization.

The knowledge I gained from learning to surround myself with business-savvy people helped to awaken the entrepreneur inside me. So goes the birthing of my consulting company: Taylor-Made International Institute, and the launching of the Women's Faith and Business Ministry.

Through the support, encouragement, and advice of women within the network, I learned the importance of bartering services and redesigning my future endeavors. This diverse group of women supported me in reshaping and restructuring my forthcoming opportunities. Watching and embracing the drive of these women pushed me to leverage my experience, touching my inner CEO gifts and talents.

I believe our drive and purpose attract much favor for discovering new relationships and new opportunities.

Women, through mutual networking and social media, who are driven, connected, and globally supportive of one another, become empowered.

I was at the beginning of my transition from employee to entrepreneur. Although I was a social media novice, I found myself forced into learning the cyberspace networking and world of business. This allowed me to attain all the world had to offer. Each of my business ventures is supported online. My life continues to be shaped through the door of new opportunities provided by social media.

Women's Faith and Business: Tying the Knot Between Ministry and the Marketplace takes advantage of social media and has become a networking butterfly. One of the biggest mistakes women make is trying to fly solo. It is okay to request assistance. Social media networking allows for an international scope of connections.

A woman who understands her purpose will always confront the status quo. A woman driven will excel and succeed in confidence. She moves from making time for what everyone else wants, to finding time for herself. She is determined to connect herself to the right women (and men) who are experiencing success, while walking in maturity and confidence. Each day she is excited about waking up with peace in her heart, health, and financial contentment. She is seriously determined to take life to a new dimension each and every day.

Through Facebook, I am profoundly moved almost every day. The connections through social media networking have opened many doors. Some of the brightest, most innovative, creative, giving, and warm people can be met through cyberspace. My virtual network has increased my net worth, not only in Tennessee, but all over the world.

Question:
Why did you feel this was a good time to do your first anthology?

Debora:

Never underestimate the value of a Facebook invite. Deeply touched by the simple idea of gratitude and affirmation from a Facebook invitation caught my attention. This introduced me to an unassuming message of gratitude and affirmation. On that day, I started a signature movement for the celebration of women and the men who served with them.

I love to honor women with encouraging inspirations, affirmations, gifts, and acts of kindness through social media and live networking events.

Women's Faith and Business: Tying the Knot Between Ministry and the Marketplace explores strategic topics, problems, and concerns to strengthen and support the efforts of women, and the men who serve in ministry and business with them. We acknowledge there can be real differences. Yet, we look for ways to complement each other through the implementation of ideas as well as connecting and supporting the women who have not found their voice in the marketplace. A faith-driven woman specializes in determination and affirmation as an advocate for her peers.

Question:
Why start this venture now?

Debora:

It was time. Through much prayer, God laid it on my heart to move forward now. With so many women in the workforce, as well as owning their own businesses, we needed to minister to each other like never before.

We are women with a call to ministry and business. We are unique and motivated to get the most out of life. My sister, you may have already accomplished a great deal in your life and may be wondering what's next. Our gifts are opportunities to embrace our chance to grow, change, and develop the authentic us. Our challenges, blunders, lessons, pitfalls, and triumphs can promote all of us into an extraordinary future. Our distinctive experiences allow us to gain knowledge through the evolution of discovery.

INTRODUCTION

In 2013, in the midst of family and ministry crises, the most devastating and agonizing transition was with the non-profit organization where I had been working for 29 years. The agency leaders lost the focus of their mission. No longer did it seem to be a safe place for productive growth as we helped others. It felt as though it had become a den of deceit on every level. I was truly thankful to God for my sweet release from my employment in July of 2013.

Why do I share this? Because when a woman is driven with a willingness to obey God for the required time, assigned in the midst of chaos, she will discover great and remarkable things about herself.

Volume 1 of the *Women's Faith and Business: Tying the Knot Between Ministry and the Marketplace* was birthed because there was something inside me that screamed, "Success." Our creative intellectual space matters to us. Reflecting on the reality that I have more life behind me than in front of me, made me realize the tick tock of each day mattered even more. Some of my greatest lessons were learned during these last couple years.

Although I had many questions, I was encouraged to enter a journey of self-fulfillment for these latter years. Slowly, and painfully, I began to regain a sense of renewed purpose. After a life-changing encounter, a small still voice spoke to me, in my spirit, telling me to stay focused and follow the wave of new opportunities being opened to me. These are the experiences that launched the Women's Faith and Business movement.

TRUSTING GOD NO MATTER WHAT

Onika Shirley

TRUSTING GOD NO MATTER WHAT

ONIKA SHIRLEY

"Trusting God No Matter What" takes you to a place of confidence, hope, and faith. It's easy to trust God when life is going well and you're experiencing prosperity, but do you have faith in the midst of life's storms? Determine to live by faith during the best and worst times of your life by trusting God no matter what.

ABOUT THIS AUTHOR

ONIKA SHIRLEY

Onika Shirley is a sponge for soaking up new information and experiences. After serving four plus years as president of the National Association of Professional Women, Greater Memphis Chapter, she is now the founder and CEO of Action Speaks Volume, Inc. Onika holds a bachelor's in business accounting and master's in business administration.

Onika's faith in God has given her an unstoppable mindset. "You can do whatever it is you want to do despite the odds against you."

Connect with this author and speaker for your next event:
Website: *http://ActionSpeaksVolum.com/*
Facebook: *http://Facebook.com/ActionSpeaksVolume/*
Email: *ActionSpeaksVolume@gmail.com*

More from Onika Shirley
   Women We Must Stand Strong
   Her Prayers "Prayers for the Deeply Wounded"
   Purpose Shakers: Women Who Rise to the Call of Purpose
      "Purpose Driven, No Matter What!"

Available Services
   Confidence and Action Coaching
   Financial Fitness Consulting
   Inspirational/Motivational Speaking (life skills and
      procrastination)
   Confidence Building for Every Women and Every Girl
   Action Takers Mentoring Program

Trusting God No Matter What

Onika Shirley

Trust in him at all times; ye people, pour out your heart before him: God is a refuge for us.

—Psalm 62:8 KJV

God is truth. He can be trusted, no matter what. He is light on the dark path of life; he is strength and salvation. We can learn so much about God and his abilities through his Word. The Word of the Lord tells us the truth. As we read the Word of God, we uncover so many examples of God's presence in the lives of others. These examples give us hope because "God is no respecter of persons" (Acts 10:34 KJV). He did it back then in the Bible for Job; I know he can do the same for us today. His Word gives us something to look forward to even when circumstances are less than promising.

In the Word, we see that God fulfills his promises and he does what he says he is going to do. Looking at the lives of others, life can be threatening and sometimes disappointing. However, God is a protector. We can trust him to cause us no harm. As you are faced with threatening situations, remind yourself often that God is your protector. He was not just a protector of Job, but he is your protector too. The enemy does not stand a chance when God is on your side.

As you deepen in your walk with the Lord, it is vital that you understand the weapons he has provided for you. When you take up these weapons and face your enemy with the strength of the Lord on your side, you will win every battle.

The choice is yours. I encourage you to choose to trust him no matter what.

The opposite holds true when we choose not to trust God. We walk in fear, doubt, and unbelief. When we are living our lives with a lack of trust in God, life can be very challenging and difficult, as well as it affects the lives of those we love. We're always questioning everything and everybody and we drain ourselves trying to do everything ourselves versus accepting the assistance we could have. Because we lack the skills and the strength, the strain can cause us to stagnate, but God is our provider and he is our protector. God is omniscient and he is omnipresent.

Alone, we do not have the necessary power to confront the evil forces that stand against us daily, but God does. Think about all the people and negativity against us every day. Yes, these forces are unwanted, unannounced, and sometimes unbearable. We need God because we can't protect ourselves in our own strength. We have to deal with jealous people, selfish people, evil people; natural circumstances, our own temptations, and our own weaknesses. The word of God tells us that he is powerful. When we have faith in who he is and what he is capable of doing, we will experience a better life and have better success in our businesses and lives. So open your eyes and ears, and allow God to do what he does so well—lead and guide along the path to victory. He is the light in dark places. "Do not be wise in your own eyes; fear the Lord and shun evil" (Proverbs 3:7 NIV).

Three Ways to Trust God No Matter What

I want to bring your attention to three ways to trust God no matter what. Firstly, establish a relationship with God; secondly, be patient with the timing of God; and lastly, understand the concept of God. Once you understand who God is, you will be able to trust him, accept his ways, and desire to do his will versus your own. With all my heart, I pray you learn, as I have, that when you trust God, you don't have to worry, fret, or doubt when traveling the road of life. God is right there with you.

Establish a Relationship with God

Relationships are vital to human experiences. They are the reason we exist. Without these connections, life seems to lose its savor. Life can be lonely, stressful, and sometimes disappointing. We tend to thrive more in life when we establish loving, peaceful, and trusting associations. When the bond is right and the foundation is strong, people look forward to the union they have established with loved ones, friends, co-workers, neighbors, strangers, and rivals. Above all others, I have found one relationship most crucial to our very being.

Our relationship with God is the one we can't afford to live without. According to Romans 6:23, the cost of sin is death; that makes life without the Creator very expensive. When we establish a relationship with God, we're able to effectively engage in relationships with others in the face of drawbacks, conflicts, and problems.

Establishing solid relationships require us to let go of our selfishness. We have to give up some things. We have to let go of doing what we want, when we want, the way we want, because in relationships, there are other people to consider. Maintaining these bonds require us to give up some of our time, our space, and our stuff. Yes, it is an ongoing struggle to keep relationships in good standing. The same struggle is also true with God. We desire a meaningful connection with our Creator, but we still want to do things our own way. We are selfish and we want to live in sin. I can almost hear God saying, "Not in my space will I allow you to do any and every thing." God's Word says, "Be holy, because I am holy" (1 Peter 1:16 NIV).

Sometimes people wait because they feel they don't have what it takes to be in a relationship with God, but there's no special formula, no hidden agendas, and no temporary passwords to start a satisfying life with God. You only need to speak to him with a humble prayer of faith. Your words don't have to be eloquent or extravagant. Speak to God from your heart. Tell him you want to get to know him. Tell him you want to follow his plan for your life. Tell him you're willing to follow his will and his timing rather than yours.

When I choose to rejoice in God, even when life goes wrong, I feel so much better, no matter what had happened. I am only able to run to my comforter because I know him and he knows me. We have a relationship, and it is simply like no other. When we feel forsaken, we can hold on to God. Habakkuk tells us to, "Trust God no matter what."

I know you are wondering what to do when everything you're counting on seems to suddenly fall apart. What do you do when life disappoints you? What do you do when your business fails? What do you do when your relationships with other people break apart? My advice to you is to trust God and keep on trusting him, no matter what!

Patience is Necessary When You Trust God

Do you create some of your own battles? Sometimes our lives are harder because of our own inability (and often flat out refusal) to wait on God. God is the strong tower. If you're trying to live your life without trusting him, you *will* fail.

Without God, you are limited, but with God there are no limits. Try to rely and totally trust him to be your strength and power along the way.

Many people make the mistake of attempting to do everything on their own, but life is so much easier when you are walking with God. Others find they have the mind to do a thing, but no patience for the time it will take to get it done. God's timing is different from our timing, so if you're trying to make things happen now and without God, you *will* fail. Your own timing is seldom correct. You will be either too late or too early, but God's timing is always perfect.

Think about the times you have made a wrong decision. When you walk, operate, and think on your own, you're subject to go down the wrong path. In the past, perhaps you have tried to figure out the solution to problems in your life, but the real answer can only be found in Christ. When you trust God, he can strengthen your faith in him. Your faith needs strengthening so you can grow—we are to live by faith and not by sight.

It is important to know that waiting on God is an act of faith. Personal experience has shown me that God will not stretch us beyond our capabilities and he doesn't allow questions that need to be answered, to go unanswered. Sometimes, we need to trust and obey, unquestioningly. "Trust in the Lord with all your heart; do not depend on your own understanding" (Proverbs 3:5 NLT). Yes, God is an unorthodox being. You may not see him working on your situation, but he is right there. You can trust him through his Word. You can trust him on what he said and what he is still saying. He will not allow you to leave this earth without fulfilling everything he has planned for your life.

God had plans for you even before you were formed in your mother's womb. Don't pretend to have it all together when you're sitting in his presence—he already knows all about you. He knows your deepest secrets. Nothing is hidden. He is not expecting you to solve the problems that arise before you. He wants you to come to him. He wants you to realize you need him and that he can be trusted. God simply wants you to hear and obey his commandments without hesitation. He wants you to trust him. When you follow God's plan and his will, he'll do the rest. God has promised to supply all your needs; however, you must learn to take him at his word. You may be feeling that it's easier said than done, but I have tried him for myself. I'm a living witness that you can trust God no matter what! In spite of the circumstance, trust God. In spite of the situation, trust God. In spite of the odds against you, trust God.

The enemy is not going to allow you to wait patiently and be free from distraction. Nobody said the road would be easy, but when you travel the road with God, all things are possible. Many people and things will come against you once you decide to lean on the Lord; however, choosing to trust God, no matter what your eyes might see or your ears might hear, will increase your faith that he is indeed by your side. Now, be courageous. Be bold. Be strong. And in the process, know that God is always in control.

Our inability to wait on God causes us to incur unnecessary challenges and disappointments, but when we turn it over to God, he has a way of working it for our good. Challenges and disappointments are a part of this life, but the key is trusting God to navigate you through the rough terrain.

Whether facing distractions from the happy life you had planned, sickness in your body, or loss of a loved one, God is the answer to all your issues. Won't you reach out to him and trust his Word? During these times, the enemy will constantly remind you of what was and what could have been. When you allow the enemy time and space, he will create fear and worry, but God wants to help you. Will you trust him? God wants to empower you to trust him no matter what. The Word of God tells us, in 2 Corinthians 12:9, that his grace is sufficient, and his strength is made perfect in our weakness. When things are not happening at the time or in the manner you had hoped, trust God. The valley may be dark and God's timing may not be your timing, but know with God you can walk through the valley victoriously.

Recite the Following Declarations to Help You Trust God When You Feel Impatient
I surrender all that I am.
I surrender all that I have.
I choose today to turn away from my thoughts.
I choose today to forget my timing and my will.
I need your help Lord.
I need you to strengthen my mind.
Empower me to trust you no matter what.
Empower me to see my weakness is your strength.
I choose to be patient.
I choose to follow the Word of the Lord.
I know your timing is better than my timing.
I know your ways are not my ways.
Lord, I trust you.
I trust you with everything I have.
I trust you with my life, no matter what!

When you trust God you will experience freedom. You will no longer need to be locked up in your own mind. You will no longer have to fear tomorrow, and you will no longer have to try to figure out the answer to a problem you will never fully solve. You have a helper. Will you trust him? Be patient and trust God. Stop, be still, and follow the direction of the Lord.

Actions You Can Take to Begin to Trust God
1. Forgive all who have wronged you or those whom you feel have failed you at any point in your life.
2. Don't blame God for past failures.
3. Communicate with God in prayer and trust him no matter what.
4. Ask God to forgive you and heal you from any past hurts and pain.
5. Draw a positive image of God in your mind and in your heart.
6. Stop believing the lies of the enemy.
7. Confess with your mouth that you are going to trust God no matter what.
8. Ask God to help you understand his character.
9. Read the Word of God daily.
10. Stop making excuses.

Once you have established a relationship of trust with God, you are ready for your abundant life of promise because God is so faithful to his Word. Once and for all you can lose all the doubt you may have had. He is going to come through for you just as he said. He really wants you to believe in his promises. When things don't look good with your physical eyes, open your spiritual eyes, and watch God work things out for your good. The process of believing starts in your head, so replace all negative thoughts with positive thoughts. Your thoughts are very powerful. Trust God with your whole life and all the problems within it. "Many are the afflictions of the righteous, but the Lord delivers him out of them all." (Psalm 34:19 NASB).

What It Means to Trust God
Remember the acronym T - R - U - S - T.

Trust God at all times and with all things.

Rest your mind by giving all your cares to God.

Understand God is in control.

Surrender to God.

Turn from your doubting ways and trust God for his best.

Affirmation

I will trust in the Lord at all times.

I will trust in the Lord going in.

I will trust in the Lord coming out.

I will trust him with my mind.

I will trust him with my body.

I will trust him with my soul.

I will trust the Lord, no matter what.

As with any relationship, it is key that you know, like, and trust the individual. Whether on your job, in your own business, or some type of dealings you may have aside from your ministry, how likely are you to engage in business with someone you don't know, don't like, and don't trust? Not likely at all. We know in the business world that those three elements are necessary for productive endeavors. God is asking no less of us. The only difference is that God will never con you. His Word is true all the time. If you have been following what I have been saying, you now have a great start to establishing a relationship with God and like any other relationship, it is critical to know, like, and trust the person in order to be willing to follow them. Your relationships require actions. Read God's Word and pray daily. You will learn and know his ways. Once you know him, I am certain you will like him. The more you like him, the easier it will be to trust him. Relationships require communication, they require you to be a good listener, and they require time. Just as you must in your business, are you willing to take the necessary actions to establish a relationship with God? Are you willing to choose to trust him no matter what?

Reinforcing the Knot —&—

- You must decide to trust God no matter what.
- When you trust God as you face your worse calamity, you will discover God is faithful to his Word.
- A relationship with God is the most important relationship you will ever have.

SOLDIERS OF THE MARKETPLACE, "RISE UP!"

Mattie Shannon

SOLDIERS OF THE MARKETPLACE, "RISE UP!"

MATTIE SHANNON

As marketplace soldiers of the gospel, not only are we called to win lost souls until Jesus returns, but also to impact the marketplace with God's presence and glory. Marketplace soldiers, it's time to rise up!

ABOUT THIS AUTHOR

MATTIE SHANNON

Elder Mattie Shannon's first love is her Lord. Her next love is her husband, Minister Ronnie Shannon, her children and grandchildren.

Mattie, a life-long learner, has earned a Master of Science in human services and worked in criminal justice for eleven years. As an ordained elder, she is now working on a master's degree in theology.

As the founder of Daughter of Zion, a ministry designed to fortify women by rebuilding their lives toward spiritual wholeness through the Word of God, Mattie has shared the Word of God and countless victories over her own personal adversities.

With a mission to spiritually boost women in mind, body, and spirit, Mattie is an inspiring and motivating speaker, who's not afraid to share the burning passion from her heart.

Connect with this author and speaker for your next event:
Website: *www.ADemonSlayerRoseUpOutOftheFire.com*
Twitter: *Woman Warrior 7*
Email: *MattieShannon35@gmail.com*

More from Mattie Shannon (pen name: Woman Warrior)
   A Demon Slayer Rose Up Out of The Fire

Available Services
   Motivational Speaking for:
      Women's Conventions * Church Organizations *
      Criminal Justice Facilities * Twelve-Step Programs

SOLDIERS OF THE MARKETPLACE, "RISE UP!"

Mattie Shannon

For our struggle is not against flesh and blood, but against the rulers, against the authorities, against the powers of this dark world and against the spiritual forces of evil in the heavenly realms.

—Ephesians 6:12 NIV

Every branch of the armed services has specific core values for each soldier. As soldiers in God's army, should we do any less for the kingdom of God? Soldiers, it's time to rise up and take a stand. Your time has come to walk in the fullness of your purpose, destiny, and potential. God is calling forth his soldiers—those that have been hiding behind the walls of their homes, warming the pews in the churches, and cowering in their cubicles on their jobs. God wants to send forth his soldiers to go into the marketplace, scout out new territory, and reclaim what's his. God says it's time to give Satan and his minions their eviction notice.

You are kingdom soldiers. You are called to operate in various areas in the marketplace, and be living examples of God's qualities. You are called to exercise your God-given skills, authority, and power in the marketplace using wisdom and knowledge to work in the vineyard (marketplace) strategically as you gather lost souls for the kingdom of God. Before we go further, let's be clear on what is meant by marketplace. The marketplace could be your cubicle on your job, your business, or anywhere you conduct business whether it be a brick and mortar establishment or online. That is your marketplace. As a soldier, be a spreader of God's Word and meet the people where they are. These may be the people who live next door or the ones who work next door to your office. They are people who might not be inclined to come into God's house to get his Word.

God uses soldiers in his army that fit his qualifications to fight on the combat field. Each kingdom soldier has been trained and equipped to operate in many positions, with an array of functions, duties, and responsibilities. So, what are the positions of these soldiers?

Soldiers of the Gospel

This is God's great commission to us, "Therefore, go and make disciples of all the nations, baptizing them in the name of the Father and the Son and the Holy Spirit. Teach these new disciples to obey all the commands I have given you. And be sure of this: I am with you always, even to the end of the age" (Matthew 28:19-20 NLT). Being foot soldiers, soldiers of the gospel, spreading and sharing God's Word to those that are blinded, lost, sick, and confused is a mandate to aid in his plan to redeem humanity.

A soldier's earthly mission is to share God's Word fearlessly. Even so, avoid being a drill sergeant; but don't be afraid to let it flow into the midst of everyday conversations, as you move about in your marketplace. Allow God's word to speak for itself. Soldiers of the gospel should have Holy Ghost boldness and courage to go through this world of darkness, not hesitating or fearful in the face of actual or possible danger. Soldiers should strive to proceed firmly on a course of divine action in spite of difficulty or opposition.

Rise up and be ready to share God's word with everyone in the marketplace through personal interactions. God has called and empowered his foot soldiers to be his witnesses to those who do not yet know him (Matthew 4:19 and Acts 1:6 NIV).

Soldiers of War

In this time period called the 21st century, there's a battle in the marketplace between the heavenly kingdom and the kingdom of darkness. The battleground is where lost souls gather and dwell daily. It is a place where the harvest is fruitful, ripe, and ready for the picking.

As mighty marketplace soldiers, God has given you great authority and power to march into unknown territory (the marketplace) and bring all things into captivity and submission unto him. Turn that hostile ground into a fertile ground. Your duty, as kingdom soldiers, is to subdue the enemy and take charge. Although you may have to declare war, it doesn't mean a violent battle. Yes, you are a soldier, but you are also a peacemaker. You can win a war without uttering a word. Your, quiet, consistent, Christ-like behavior may be all you need to change and win over your entire office or neighborhood.

Pray daily. It's our God-given mission to cast out demons and heal the sick. Are you bold enough to believe you can raise the dead? Your mere presence of God's anointing can prevail over darkness in the lives of the people and situations in the marketplace. God has called and equipped his kingdom soldiers, through the Holy Spirit, to actively influence the marketplace. The goal is to turn lost souls to the risen Savior.

Every man and every woman has a God-given gift. Use it to his glory. Use your gifts, talents, skills, and abilities for the glory of God. Man, woman, young, or old, there is a place for you in God's army. Only you can fill that role. No mission is more important than another is. Fulfill your assignment. Obey God.

Soldiers of the Harvest

The marketplace is where many people spend the majority of their time. This creates a great opportunity to share God's Word in those daily encounters with co-workers, employees, customers, patients, clients, and even supervisors. Call it your marketplace pulpit to the world.

Indeed God has given us his great commission to take the gospel to the entire world. The Bible also says for us to be wise as serpents but harmless as doves. In other words, use common sense in your approach. Speak at the appropriate times. Use wisdom. If your office has a policy about Christian materials and conversations, abide by it. I'm sure you've heard the saying that you can catch more flies with honey than with vinegar—it works for the kingdom soldier as well. It's hard to win people if you annoy them. Use a wiser approach; conduct yourself with integrity. Let them see an example of someone doing the right things at the right times. Show them the love of God. Be kind. Be patient. Work as unto the Lord. Be an example of all things right. Be a good listener. Speak as God gives you knowledge. Speak when asked and at the correct times such as lunch and other breaks or after hours. If you are on your job, it's not likely you're being paid to "win souls." Doing anything other than what you are hired to do is stealing from your employer. That's not a good witness.

Live your life in such a compelling way that others come to you, ready to hear a word from the Lord. Stand for what you know is right, but don't be obnoxious about it. Pray, pray, and pray some more. Be a wise soldier and use a little honey.

God knows and understands that many lost souls may never step into an actual church, but they go to work, shopping malls, supermarkets, and the like. So, what are we to do? We can bring the church to the people and meet them where they are. God wants his soldiers of gospel to shine as lights in places where darkness has dwelt for so long. Be ready. Be available.

There are so many lost souls in need of the Savior. God has given us our marching orders. We are to go forth and gather the harvest. They are out there, waiting on us. With wisdom and tenderness, gather those lost ones. Leave no stone unturned.

The Soldier's Designer Armor

God didn't make clones. He wants us as unique as the rest of his creation. God has one army, but many soldiers. As soldiers in God's army, the uniforms for battle may differ greatly. Some of us may have skinny leg jeans and a rhinestone T-shirt. Others may be wearing exclusive designer two-piece suits with all the extras. Still others are wearing scrubs, and chef hats with matching aprons, or mechanic uniforms. We're all in the same army.

Ladies, God has issued his soldiers new battle gear. Our outward appearance is fresh, updated, and stylish, yet the foundation of our armor remains steadfast and sure. Don't leave home half-dressed.

Wear the full armor of God. Wear God's armor so that you can fight against the devil's clever tricks. Our fight is not against people on earth. We are fighting against the rulers and authorities and the powers of this world's darkness. We are fighting against the spiritual powers of evil in the heavenly places. That is why you need to get God's full armor. Then on the day of evil, you will be able to stand strong. And when you have finished the whole fight, you will still be standing. So stand strong with the belt of truth tied around your waist, and on your chest wear the protection of right living. On your feet wear the Good News of peace to help you stand strong. And also use the shield of faith with which you can stop all the burning arrows that come from the Evil One. Accept God's salvation as your helmet. And take the sword of the Spirit—that sword is the teaching of God. Pray in the Spirit at all times. Pray with all kinds of prayers, and ask for everything you need. To do this you must always be ready. Never give up. Always pray for all of God's people.

—Ephesians 6:11–18 ERV

There is no substitute for daily prayer. This keeps you in communion with Jesus Christ, our commander-in-chief. Prayer causes us to learn when it's time to move forward. Prayer protects us while we war with the enemy, being careful, not to become a casualty of war.

Yes, we are looking good and dressed in style on the outside, but underneath; we are still warriors, dressed in full battle gear.

Soldiers of Salt

As soldiers of salt in the marketplace, we are to represent purity, honesty, and loyalty. We should create a thirst and hunger for the things of God. As soldiers of salt, we are to bring hope and excitement to the lives of God's people. We must not allow evil to diminish or destroy the moral fiber of society and allow it to be made impure by the exposure of the enemy's darkness. God wants us to continuously watch and pray until the day our Lord and Savior, Jesus Christ, returns.

Although earthly salt will dissolve in water, as a soldier of salt, we realize, and understand, that we are not of this world, but visitors passing through to our eternal home (John 15:19 NIV). We will not melt from the rain of adversity.

Salt can endure extreme heat. As soldiers of salt, so should we—no matter what the world throws at us or puts us through, we should still maintain our flavor. However, if we mix with the things of this world and become influenced by the deceitful riches and material cares of this world, then we could be destroyed by our own selfish desires and temptations. God's soldiers of salt are his rainbow to the people in the marketplace. Unfortunately, there is no promise of a pot of gold at the end of the rainbow; but, there is healing, hope, deliverance, and freedom.

With this great and awesome manifestation of the mighty love of God in the atmosphere, let's begin to create a thirst not for natural water, but the living water, Jesus Christ. As soldiers of salt, we know only Jesus Christ can quench the thirst of the unbeliever. We should create an insatiable appetite and hunger, not for natural food, but for spiritual food–the Word of God.

Soldiers of the Light

As soldiers of light for God (Matthew 5:14 NIV), we bring the truth of God into the marketplace to those who are lacking spiritual insight. We are to provide them with strong and confident expectations toward a positive and productive life in God.

Through us, the soldiers of the light, God extends his love to those who feel their lives have no meaning. God shows his love, often through us, to those that no one remembers or cares about their earthly existence. Yes, he loves those who feel no one holds any deep affection toward them or cherishes them at all. He especially loves those who are unable to think with clarity or act with understanding and intelligence.

God's light within us should shine so brightly before the world, that it draws all mortals to him. To be an agent of change, this is God's purpose for you in the marketplace.

Just as Jesus came to do in his earthly ministry, so are we to declare freedom for the captives as God restores them to a healthy mind and body. Yes, we are bringing God's glory to those who are in dire need of it.

Soldiers of Authority

As God's soldiers of authority, God has equipped us with his dunamis power (divine strength) and authority to influence the marketplace and saturate this arena with Christlikeness.

Soldiers of authority, you have been called, anointed, and appointed to take dominion and authority in your homes and in the marketplace. God wants you to make disciples for his kingdom (Matthew 28:16–20 NIV).

We build relationships through daily interactions such as casual conversations with employees, delivery people, cooks or waitresses in the restaurant, homeless men or women on the corner, salespersons, a woman pushing her baby in a stroller on the public sidewalk or in the mall. Doors of opportunities, through ordinary conversations, could swing wide open to draw lost souls to God. Soldier, you might be the one to lead those who have walked away in the past to now come back to God.

Soldiers of Lost Souls

God wants his soldiers of lost souls to be completely sold out to him. He wants us fully surrendered and dedicated to him physically, mentally, financially, and spiritually for the kingdom. God wants his soldiers to be readily available to penetrate the marketplace with power and tenacity. God wants his soldiers to possess the ability to fight spiritually and the wisdom to know when to stand still and watch God work. We need to possess the wisdom to know when to plan a strategic attack and rescue the lost. The closer you draw to God, the more you will see these abilities come alive in your own life.

Remember, soldiers of lost souls, you may be the only opportunity others have to see and experience the Savior. That is why it is vital to show God's love and compassion to those you meet in the marketplace. Think about it—someone could be lost for all eternity simply because you chose not to answer God's call. That's not a pretty thought.

God will hold you accountable for not seizing the chance to bring lost souls into his kingdom. Your life is not your own. Your life kingdom work is to win lost souls for God. You cannot force people to accept Jesus, but you can 'live' Jesus before them.

By the age of twelve, Jesus was about the business of both his earthly and his heavenly fathers (Luke 2:49 NIV). For his earthly father (Joseph), Jesus did carpentry work. For his heavenly Father (God), Jesus conducted the most powerful ministry ever. Jesus was being obedient to both, in the natural and spiritual realms; and you too, have been called to operate in the natural and spiritual realm, as Jesus did.

God wants you, his soldiers in the marketplace, to ignite the burning fire that lies deep within your heart. You are in the marketplace to win lost souls for the kingdom of God. Satan's mission is to prevent lost souls from leaving his kingdom of darkness. He will use everything he has to prevent any soul from walking into the kingdom of God. We are soldiers. Our mission is to bring lost souls into the light.

Soldiers of Preservation

As soldiers of preservation, God has ordered and commanded us to keep and sustain the earth (Genesis 1:28 NIV). Yes, God has called us as soldiers to preserve by supporting the laws and policies that align with God's standards.

The marketplace is a battle zone between heaven and the kingdom of darkness. That's why it's so important that we, his soldiers in the marketplace, should continuously be geared up with the whole armor of God for protection and ready for battle (Ephesians 6:10–18 NIV).

Conclusion

As soldiers, we cannot confine ourselves within the church walls. We are soldiers; it's time to go to the battlefield. The battlefield can be our neighborhood, homes, schools, and yes, even the marketplace. We are soldiers in God's mighty army. We are soldiers of the kingdom. Soldier, it's time to rise up. God has called, anointed, and appointed you to go out into new territory to spread his message of hope. God is calling for soldiers to proclaim his Word to those that may never otherwise hear the gospel. God, strategically, has placed his children in positions of entrepreneurship as well as leadership in Fortune 500 companies. We are employed in hospitals, banks, restaurants, clothing stores, stadiums—nearly every marketplace imaginable—we are there.

Wherever God has placed you in the marketplace, as a soldier, you have a mission to fulfill. You have been trained for battle and equipped to work in the marketplace to win lost souls and bring out those that are spiritually blind, lame, sick, impoverished, and dead. If you have been planting seeds along the way, the harvest is now ripe, fertile, and ready for picking.

Consciously be aware that you are in a combat zone. You are battling for lost souls against the kingdom of darkness. The enemy is not going to allow you to freely walk out of the marketplace with souls he believes are his own. Remember, as kingdom soldiers, you are effective and powerful soldiers of the gospel, sharing God's words with all those who will listen.

Soldiers of war, yes, equipped with mighty spiritual weapons to take down and destroy the enemy. We are soldiers of the harvest, gathering lost souls for the kingdom of God. We are soldiers of salt, seasoning society with his words. We are soldiers of light, being God's visible light in the midst of darkness. We are soldiers of authority, exercising dunamis power, through prayer, over all that go against God's laws and commands. We are soldiers of lost souls, guiding those who lack spiritual direction to the Savior. We are soldiers of preservation, protecting society and keeping its moral fiber intact with God's intended original state for humanity.

To whom it may concern, the memo has gone out. The workers of darkness don't stand a chance. They might as well stand down now, because God's soldiers are about to rise up— the victory is already ours.

Reinforcing the Knot

- Live your life in such a compelling way that others come to you, ready to hear a word from the Lord.
- Stand for what you know is right, but don't be obnoxious about it. Pray, pray, and pray some more.
- Be a wise soldier and use a little honey.

LET YOUR LIGHT SHINE

Evangelane Turner

LET YOUR LIGHT SHINE

EVANGELANE TURNER

It is not always easy to let your light shine when all seems so dark. "Let Your Light Shine" is a synopsis of three steps to a bright, positive, and productive life in Christ—in spite of the dark clouds. The best way to remove darkness is to turn on the light.

About this Author

Evangelane Turner

Evangelane Turner is a well-educated woman of God with a big heart for others. She holds a bachelor's in social services along with a master's in leadership. She didn't stop there, her concern for others has led her to pursue a master's in clinical mental health counseling as well.

A seasoned, licensed minister and faith-based counselor, Evangelane has led several support groups in areas such as grief and recovery, marital healing, and family restoration. She is the founder of Heart to Heart Ministries, Inc., but mentoring in a singles ministry has allowed her to bring out her fun side.

Connect with this author and speaker for your next event:
Facebook: *Evangelane Turner*
Email: *Evangelane.Turner@gmail.com*

Available Services
Heart to Heart Ministries, Inc. (founder)

LET YOUR LIGHT SHINE

Evangelane Turner

Let your light so shine before men, that they may see your good works and glorify your Father in heaven.
—Matthew 5:16 NKJV

Step One: Love God

It is important to put God first in everything we do. This makes us pleasing in his sight. Obedience causes everything else to fall into place—according to God's will for our lives. God is the reason we live, move, and have our being. We are to give him all the glory and honor due to him. We must spend quality time in his presence. I like to worship, pray, and read God's Word in my devotional time with God. It's been said that God's gift to us is our life. What we do with our life is our gift to God. Let's make that gift count by making a difference in this world and being a bright light in a dark world.

We should be confident God hears our prayers, knowing that all things will work out because we belong to him and he belongs to us. When you find yourself in a dark place in your life, just know that God loves you. Focus on the good things that he has in store for you and know that he has a purpose and a plan for your life. Stay focused on God's love for you no matter how dark it seems right now.

Step Two: Love Yourself

Loving yourself means forgiving yourself from all the old mistakes and hurts. It means letting go of all the fears and anxieties of the past. Give yourself permission to be free to live and love again. Jesus came to earth so we could live freely and abundantly. Don't deprive yourself of that freedom because you are stuck in the past. Let it go and be free.

Loving yourself also means finding your true identity and life purpose. Become that person God designed you to be. Discover your destiny. You are destined for greatness, so develop yourself by setting both short and long-term goals. Get whole in the areas that are broken—whether it is your credit, weight, finances, or spirituality; it doesn't matter what area it is, as long as you get the proper help in order to reach your desired goal. Be the best version of you because you're awesome.

Love yourself by letting your light shine wherever you are. Your light goes where you go because the light is in you. Be free and enjoy life. Wherever you go and whatever you do, always remain positive and productive.

Another way to love yourself is by pampering yourself and having fun. I like to treat myself to pedicures, manicures, and massages. I spoil myself because I am worth it. I am fearfully and wonderfully made, so I have to take care of my temple. One more way that I cater to myself is by getting an ice cream cone when I reach a desired goal. I love ice cream and I indulge myself occasionally. There is nothing wrong with loving yourself. You cannot love anyone else if you don't love yourself. You teach people how to treat you by the way you treat yourself. Embrace who you are.

Step Three: Love Others

This step can sometimes be a challenge, but don't let anyone (or anything) ever dim your light. You can be in control of your emotions because God has you in the palm of his hand. This may be your most difficult test, but remember to stay focused on God's love for you. As long as you know who you are and whose you are, nothing else matters to the point of dimming your light. Shine bright in the midst of adversity. There is a light at the end of every tunnel.

Smile and be pleasant—even when others are not. I have learned that sometimes people have simply had a bad day and they don't mean any harm. Most of the time, it is not even about us. Sometimes people just need a hug or a word of encouragement. We can be that light that they need at that moment. Loving others can be very rewarding. Often times, if we are having a bad day, loving others can turn our dark place into a bright place. Loving others is actually loving God and yourself because God is love.

When I come into my workplace and the atmosphere is gloomy and stuffy, I refuse to let the grumps dampen my naturally bubbly, positive, and outgoing personality. I let the light of Jesus shine through me as I come in and greet everyone enthusiastically. The love and light of Christ, shining through me, changes the entire atmosphere. Through Christ, we have the ability to change the atmosphere with our light. The way to remove darkness is by letting our light shine. Darkness flees when light is present.

An Important Part of the Process: Be Yourself

Be yourself. Never try to impress anyone or pretend to be someone you are not. Realize that not everyone is going to like you, but it is their loss. Be the person God created you to be. Live freely and without regrets. Embrace who you are and use your gifts and talents to make the world a better place. You don't have to travel around the globe. Simply put: bloom where you are planted. You can start right where you are. You may want to start a Bible study or serve in your local church or help feed the homeless. Whatever you do, do it as unto God and not man.

My Testimony

I accept the fact that not everyone is going to fall in love with my exuberant personality. For some personality types, my daily excitement is actually quite annoying. However, because I know who and whose I am, I can rise above the bad attitudes of others. My goal is to treat everyone with love and kindness because God is love. I'm not saying that I don't get upset at times, we all do. My only solution is to turn every situation over to God.

Being a light in a dark place is hardly an easy task. However, it is worth every effort. God always sees me through it. There is always light at the end of the tunnel. I have laughed and I have cried, but God always elevates me in due season.

Let your light shine and be you because no one can outdo you being you. Don't change yourself to suit the whims of others. Be you. Be authentic. Be original. Be true to yourself. Letting your light shine means being the best version of you.

I am embracing who I am. I have come to the place where I love myself unconditionally. I am proud of who I am. I know who and whose I am. I know my life purpose. I have been through a lot of pain, but I am an overcomer. I have survived divorce and abuse (physical, verbal, emotional). I have learned to love myself and let my light shine. Love the skin you are in and never let anyone dull your sparkle.

I have been married three times. The first two marriages were abusive. The third marriage was a case of two prideful, hotheaded people that were selfish and didn't have enough sense to work out the marriage. I can laugh about it now, but the truth is the truth. We later discussed it and apologized for individual parts in the divorce. Today, we are still great friends. In the midst of all this darkness, a passion to restore marriages God's way was birthed.

I found something out about myself. As the saying goes, "I was looking for love in all the wrong places." I was looking for a man to love me instead of me loving myself. What I overlooked was that God already loved me. He loved me then and He loves me now. God's love is unconditional. Love is not based on how you feel or if you act a certain way. Love is so much more than being with a man. Love is a choice. God is love. Real love will love you to life. Love is not in a hurry. Love allows you to be yourself and allows you to thrive and be free. Love is not bondage nor is it controlling. Love knows no limit to its endurance, no end to its trust, and no fading of its hope. Love can outlast anything. Love still stands when all else has fallen. God is Love. I choose God.

After my last divorce, I didn't think that I could make it alone or even breathe. Well, I am breathing and I am doing better than I ever have. It is funny how a dark place can cause a person to shine brighter than ever before. I went on to get a bachelor's degree, a master 's degree, and a certificate in human resource. I even started working on a second master's degree. I am also the founder of a non-profit organization, Heart To Heart Ministries, designed to help encourage, strengthen, and empower others to free themselves from the snares of the enemy and be who they are destined to be. In a nutshell, never let anyone dull your sparkle, a dark place can cause you to shine brighter than ever before, and never change because a naysayer does not like who you are. Shine.

Reinforcing the Knot ⎯⊗⎯
- Stay focused on God's love for you no matter how dark it seems.
- Embrace who you are and be the best version of you because you're awesome.
- Remove darkness by letting your light shine. Darkness flees when light is present.

B.U.T. IN DUE SEASON

Cynthia King

B.U.T. in Due Season

Cynthia King

Many are called, but few have answered. Some are called to the pulpits; yet others are called to find their niche in the marketplace. For those called to the marketplace, there is a relentless, inward battle. The clash is launched between faith-based standards versus worldly business practices that push to make a profit at all cost.

Though we are pressed on every side, we will not fail. The call must be answered. We must battle until triumph (B.U.T.) and know that it will all come in due season.

ABOUT THIS AUTHOR

CYNTHIA KING

Cynthia King, a long-time resident of Memphis, TN, holds a bachelor's degree in business. After nearly, thirty years of employment with a major air freight carrier, she became CEO of her own business which she named Ah-Sensational. Ah-Sensational is devoted to making your special events the talk of the town (in a good way). As for Cynthia's floral creations, they are simply Ah-Sensational.

This dynamic entrepreneur is also the owner of her own travel consultant business: Empowerment Travel.

Having worked in both the mental health and the justice arenas, she continues to motivate, serve, and inspire others in her community.

Connect with this author and speaker for your next event:
Facebook: *Ah-Sensational Floral and Events*
Email: *GreatKoncepts@outlook.com*

Available Services
> Motivational Speaking
> Event Planning
> Floral Creations
> Travel Consultant

B.U.T. in Due Season
(Battle Until Triumph)

Cynthia King

And he [Jacob] went in also unto Rachel, and he loved also Rachel more than Leah, and served with him [Laban] yet seven other years.

—Genesis 29:1–35, 30:11 KJV

Tying the knot between faith and the marketplace has been in existence for over two thousand years. Though books have been written, no one covers it more fully than the Bible. People question whether faith belongs in the marketplace. This question can be answered by considering that Christ engaged in commerce—turning fishermen into disciples. Even hanging on the cross, he 'paid the wages' for man's sins. The Romans gambled for his garments. As you read through the chapters contained in this book, examine your own life. Has God called you to be a marketplace missionary? If you are a believer and God has assigned you to a position in the marketplace, no doubt he has called you to be a missionary right where you are.

The marketplace missionary is as powerful as any pulpit. Though your character will be tested daily, a new passion to serve God, while making a profit, will be established. You may enter into a divine contract that is prosperous and fulfilling. However, when built incorrectly the labor could be long and unfruitful. The clash between Rachel and Leah, in Bible, expresses this battle perfectly. Using this story as the backdrop, I would like to address the following three points: the barren place, Gad, and Judah.

The Barren Place:

When opportunity knocks, be ready. God is the creator. When he gives someone a vision or invention, he intends for it to be carried out. He won't just let it die because you weren't ready. Another person may be given the opportunity to manifest it in the marketplace. How many times have you seen a commercial only to say, "I thought of that"? It's hard to give birth to a dream that no one but you can envision—yet another reason to trust God.

Let's look at Leah. She was considered the least adored. Some books called her tangled eyed (crossed eyed) or by some, tender by the eyes (from weeping). Being in the market, there will be a shredding and tearing away of your flesh. Every day you will have to look inward to the principles of your character, moral fiber, and standards. Hold fast to those principles that will keep you from cheating on your taxes, engaging in unfair labor tactics, or the use of subpar materials. Individuals and situations will come along that require you to prove your faith. As soon as you attempt to find acceptance in the marketplace, life starts to get in the way. An illness, financial pitfalls, distractions, loss of zeal for your dream, and that never-ending invitation to come back to being average. Oh, I know how it feels to give birth to an idea only to have people say how great the competition is (the Rachel). It feels like you are pregnant, yet barren of resources, vision, and initiative. There will be that moment as the crowning of your dream comes down the birth canal, your eyes will become tender from crying out for help. As you attempt to move forward there will be opposition from those closest to you. It's a testimony and test to have friends laugh at your product when they think it's good enough to photograph, but not valued enough for wages. I know this from personal experience. I was a vendor at a bridal event. A woman came across the hall and took a photo of one of my arrangements. She then asked me where I had obtained my supplies. When I refused to volunteer the information, she became irate. This is the time for you to assign value to your vision. Will you be a bargain basement markdown or a priceless gem? Your labor is in vein if the Lord does not orchestrate it. Small mindsets will cause you to take baby steps when God is preparing you for a leap of faith. There's nothing wrong with taking baby steps, particularly when you're just starting out. Eventually, God will require you to take that seemingly giant leap of faith. Even in what seems like a barren season, your integrity in your work will be on display. Are you working as unto man or God? We represent Christ in how we conduct business. Whether positively or negatively, we represent our Savior. If we take shortcuts and do poor work, pad our invoices, con people into working with us, or steal ideas from others, and do less than our best—we still represent our Savior, but in a negative light.

We have to move forward. We must stay the course. What has God called you to do? Head in that direction and don't turn around until God calls you to your next mission. Don't even think about turning back to merely daydreaming about what could be. I've tried only to find the seat on the couch had someone else's imprint, while conversations with friends were as though someone had put the movie on pause. Yes, it's difficult to get in position when you are battle weary, but I have come to bring you a word and a promise: B.U.T. (battle until triumph) in due season.

GAD:

In the marketplace, Rachel and Jacob may have seemed favored. Rachel, though beautiful, was barren. We want to look successful, but it's hard when the creditors are calling every day. It's hard when you're bringing your little brown bag for lunch not because you're trying to save money, but because you have no money. Leah was far less comely and certainly not the preferred one, but she had the ability to conceive.

Leah conceived. Her baby was now being weened and made ready to stand on his own. She did not look differently, but her position and view of herself had changed. Entering into the marketplace is like entering a race with six-inch heels. It looks easy but you are not gaining any ground due to lack of traction. In the birthing of Gad (Leah's adoptive son), Leah pronounced a troop is coming. A strong strategy and a shift in position will be influenced only by the need to be a follower of Christ. Gad is the place where the disconnection from having no marketing promotions, no business plan, and no resources will suddenly propel your business into new realms of operation. Patience is needed here more than in the barren place. The temptation is great to become restless and doubtful. I can't express how many nights I would pace the floor, or lie awake, and cry out, "God, did you forget me?" My eyes had become like Leah's. I was focusing more on what seemed like the success of my rival than the progress I was making. You can't put faith on a time clock nor can you rub a magic lamp to gain blessings. The leadership ability to take the helm and stir your business into a new realm can be frightening. Many battles of war have been lost due to lack of commitment and having a leader that lacks the knowledge to gain the support of his followers. A great leader is born from being an even greater follower. Submission and admission that one needs help, is nothing to be ashamed of. Where you have felt alone, angelic hosts now encamp every vision, dream, and relationship. Compromise is over. Soon you will possess the ability to conceive from dry areas where others have tried and failed repeatedly. Your niche and customer base will be discovered. Success becomes a motivator to wade further into developing healthy relationships. If you are not networking and using some form of social media then you are likely missing opportunities to expand globally. In Gad, you will begin to have others that will rally to spread the works of your business and provide personal references. Many believers shy away from social media; please keep in mind that the world is larger than our back doors. Due to the internet, the ability to position oneself into several different places is a reality. Supply and demand now take on a different twist. What can't sell in Alaska can be a hot seller in Atlanta. Boosting your business via a website is not an option, it's critical. If you are caught without guides, there are now business coaches that mentor from coffee shops and lawn chairs across the country. Tying the knot in the marketplace is hindered only by your lack of turning on the switch. I can't promise you that Gad is all milk and honey. But, I will say it's the middle ground for greatness as you begin to see bad situations turn into great opportunities. The midwife comes and her mission is to make sure that dream is not aborted. If you survive the foot in the back, and are being held accountable, then you have the makings of profit. Until then, that war is just beginning—B.U.T. in due season.

Judah:

When Leah gives birth to Judah, it was a declaration and an act of praise. The marketplace tying has been a challenge and a place of triumph. Your friends that woo you privately and publicly acclaim the talents of rivals no longer matter. Who didn't show up or purchase your product doesn't matter. When others turn to laugh, you are in the lead. You know that without the struggle, victory will not arrive. The process is a struggle—sometimes an outright brawl. You may have lost the house, had to hide the car from the "repo" man, eat peanut butter and jelly or order from the dollar menu, but you have to do it without losing your character, your faith, or your mind. I have learned to climb in my heavenly Daddy's lap and find rest. Your vision has been corrected and what was crossed has now been strengthened. Open wounds are healed.

Let praise be in the mouth of the believer. In the camp of the believers, you are no longer at the mercy of strangers. Your kinsman will continue to strengthen your creative nature. If you manage to make a profit, learn to manage money wisely while departing from greed. Blessings and honors will continue to overshadow the business. Set aside time to cultivate a relationship that will free you from the stress of making riches only. Judah is the season of praise. Celebrate and lift up holy hands in your place of employment. Pray over your products, provide exceptional service to the rude and unfriendly. It all belongs to God. The manifestation of due season is a reminder just like the rainbow. When given a dream, its a covenant.

It All Has a Purpose

The barren times of my life have been the proving ground of the strength of my faith. The marketplace is just one more avenue of witnessing to the believer and nonbeliever alike. Your business is now open; every decision, even down to the toothpaste and soap you use, will measure your moral compass. The flesh will have to be scaled back, for the window of opportunity is reflective and narrow. Much like the eyes of Leah, one to reflect inward and one to focus on the next step. Gad, the place where you felt alone, now changes from average to vastness. No more compromise, the expansion of God's promises is at hand. Without expectation, your faith will lay undeveloped. Every negative force, must surrender and bow down. Expectation tied around the rock of the marketplace serves the purpose of remembering who, where, and what our purpose is in the Kingdom.

I would like to thank all who have made this opportunity possible. To my family and friends, I am grateful. As the mother of one son—still putting my feet on the ground —I am running with you in mind. My hope is that this chapter has served the purpose of encouragement.

Reinforcing the Knot

- Faith takes you into the realms of God.
- Though it may tarry, success will come. Let your faith be like a dagger, and battle until triumph.
- There is no greater season than due season.

FAITH AND NONPROFIT WORK: THE PRINCIPLES AND THEIR IMPACT

Denise Darcel Wooten

Faith and Nonprofit Work: The Principles and Their Impact

Denise Darcel Wooten

Falsely assumed is the notion that managing a tax-exempt organization, in comparison to a for-profit business, requires less critical thinking, structure, and ability. The following factors are noteworthy as we consider, or reassess, one of the most rewarding professions God has made available to us, as well as its link to the secular world.

About this Author

Denise Darcel Wooten

Denise Darcel Wooten is always up for learning—whether it's canvassing the country, re-purposing furniture or expanding her gardens. Her most treasured accomplishment is facilitating the renovation of her 93-year-old home. She takes pride in foreseeing new life in objects often discarded.

Denise has enjoyed working in both public and nonprofit administration. She holds a bachelor's degree in community leadership development along with numerous certificates in project management, non-profit fundraising, and domestic violence counseling. She also writes for community and local news outlets. Although retired, Denise continues to serve in her own neighborhood's community planning. She is also a board member with three nonprofits as well as the director of the women's ministry at her church. For Denise, every day offers a fresh opportunity to gain knowledge.

Connect with this author and speaker for your next event:
Facebook: DeniseDWooten
Email: *wooten454@sbcglobal.net*

More from Denise Wooten
   Between Here and There (co-authored, T. A. Smalls)

Available Services
   Nonprofit Management Services
   Women's Ministry Planning and Event Planning
   Community Leadership Development
   Community Neighborhood Advocacy
   Grant Writing and Fund Raising

FAITH AND NONPROFIT WORK: THE PRINCIPLES AND THEIR IMPACT

Denise Darcel Wooten

From him the whole body, joined and held together by every supporting ligament, grows and builds itself up in love, as each part does its work.

—Ephesians 4:16 NIV

When tying the knot between ministry and the marketplace, one cannot overlook the essential roles of both service and stewardship. This is especially true when they are linked to the work performed within the non-profit sector. By comparison, service and stewardship in the charitable environment stand head and shoulders above what is attributed to "doing business" in the public and private spheres. For most corporations, the bottom line is equated with making a profit. While those involved in the administration of a public charity, or 501(c)(3), believe their main objective is to improve the quality of life. With that in mind, this chapter is designed to briefly discuss key elements that should be considered and put in place by any potential stakeholder who decides that the nonprofit path is the one they want to pursue.

The marketplace is where we find consumers who depend on the delivery of goods and services from others. To supply those items that are in demand is compelling. Many find it hard to ignore the desire to accommodate and reap the benefits derived from such transactions. However, when we choose to address those needs, we must always keep in the forefront of our thoughts and actions, the primary factor that rules over every measure of our work.

All things belong to God including those we serve, what we provide, and how we behave on his behalf. Therefore, how we assume our role determines if we succeed or fail. We cannot go about running God's business in any manner that does not honor and glorify him. There is a certain principle of conduct we must exhibit when we determine to do what is right and good in his name.

God trusts us with the care, development, and enjoyment of everything he owns. Just as Adam was given charge over Eden, we must see and accept our assignment as reliable administrators and managers who will perform in good faith. When God places his creations in our hands, it requires our discipline and commitment to follow all his instructions to the letter. We are not allowed to amend the rules. We give God total control over ourselves and property. Here is where we see the importance of aligning the marketplace to what we do in our ministry work. Many might see this as a conflict of interest, to mix non-secular practices into a secular environment. Usually this false way of thinking is what gets many businesses in trouble. The scriptures contain the principles of sound business fundamentals. The Bible not only offers step by step instruction, but expresses the reward gifted for doing so.

My forty years of working within this industry, as an administrator and most often as a consultant to start-ups, has afforded me a quick study of those who come ready to learn versus those who do not. I've had many opportunities to assess what it takes to succeed, or fail, by listening to the initial questions people ask. The person who instantly inquires about profits and other financial aspects, or what qualifies as a write-off on their taxes, is immediately seen as a "red flag." I have met with individuals approaching non-profit work under the assumption that as long as there is a steady flow of donors, or they know "good" people who will make great board members, they are ready to hang out their shingle. I have also sat with those who keep returning to learn the fundamentals of customer service or how to energize aged strategies that will ensure they are meeting ever-changing trends and standards. It is refreshing to witness this outlook making an appearance long before the desire to search for a site office. Some make my job quite easy while some make it a wearisome challenge.

Scripture outlines for us where the concept of faith, work, and economics come together. Tying the knot between ministry and the marketplace is not a new idea. It was the original intention of God to see that man took on the role of caretaker for this world. As Christians, we have been taught to have faith in God to supply all our needs. We cannot rely solely in our own capabilities. This surely has to include all that we would need to carry out our Lord's affairs. Materials, equipment, and human resources will be delivered when we seek God to make them available (and he agrees). As we do the work in his name, he will answer our prayers. We are charged to be obedient, accountable, and responsible for every aspect of our business. This leads to a good harvest.

Our time and talents are trusts given to us by God. We are to invest in the work that glorifies his kingdom. We ensure the outcomes that are proposed by continuously communing with the Holy Spirit. He that indwells us delights in giving us the gift of spiritual counsel. We have to be certain to treat well what God has presented us. God wants us to maintain an acute awareness of the known and unknown dynamics that might unexpectedly impact all of the things he possesses. Here is where the economic results manifest or fall short. Our discernment through the Holy Spirit provides a road map outlining sound judgment and conclusive decision making.

God made no mistake when he created and purposed everything on earth. Every aspect of his creation has been given a unique function that has stood from the point of formation until today. Each of us is held accountable to one another. There is no truer example than that which comprises the relationship portrayed in the world of business. Ephesians 4:16 NLT declares, "He makes the whole body fit together perfectly. As each part does its own special work, it helps the other parts grow, so that the whole body is healthy and growing and full of love." In all things is the love of God. Yes, God is love.

Stakeholder accountability is not limited only to those who sign payroll checks or maintain personnel records. Those representing the marketplace positions, e.g., officers, staff, administrators, vendors, granting and contract agencies, members, volunteers, and the community at large, are charged with working in tandem for the good of all. Each plays an integral role in helping the organization run smoothly and at its very best.

As mentioned earlier, many shy away from overlapping secular with non-secular activities, thinking that they are not able to institute a degree of political correctness. Nonprofit work is not always as restrictive as most would imagine. Daily business can co-exist alongside spiritual endeavors. Many faith-based institutions are now leading the way in this harmonious arrangement by effectively weaving the two entities into a seamless setting. Many provide temporal services that are undergirded with Christian beliefs. Their efforts are heralded as welcoming and appreciated places to find resources and learn about Jesus Christ. Despite symbols and openly displayed tributes honoring their declaration of faith, some nonprofits have reported impressive up-ticks in church attendance. Those who initially came only for the programs offered now find solace and shared seating among the saints. Nonprofits that do not hide their secular views and doctrines attribute this to a non-intentional, but effective outreach effort to win souls. Ministerial staff leaves the decision to participate in religious aspects solely up to their clients.

Daycare providers, wellness clinics, and domestic violence shelters are a few of the established nonprofit organizations operating within churches under the category of public charities. Nonprofit work goes hand in hand with faith work. Much of the practices taking place in established charities are a reflection of what God expects from his ambassadors.

Many of my cohorts would probably agree that operating a nonprofit can sometimes be far harder than maintaining a for-profit of similar size. There is nothing wrong with having a sincere and caring attachment to a job. As with mission work, nonprofit employment can deliver life-altering results. We have all heard the countless success stories like the community-based organization that gave participants a second chance to do better or the one offering the opportunity to learn a new skill that opened doors previously unavailable.

There are equally as many happy endings as those unhappy ones that immediately come to mind. Whichever industry you choose, the choice should never be taken lightly. Nonprofit work is demanding. Federal and local required reports must be filed, financial management activities have to be accurate, fundraising and program development should be vibrant and strategic. Succession planning must be ongoing. Agency sustainability, beyond the grant writing phase, is an obligation.

When a nonprofit is not adequately prepared, it walks a tightrope that hangs precariously over a river of quicksand. Keep in mind that a nonprofit's major obligation to the community is to improve the quality of life. Once the doors open and people begin to utilize the services offered, that nonprofit becomes a lifeline for them. Their trust and dependency on the organization living up to its mission statement sets a precedence that has a ripple effect.

When lack of funding (or other issues) causes staff reduction and closed programs, the impact is far reaching. Those who are looking for a chance to become first-time homeowners, teens attempting to find sparse summer employment, and seniors wanting to not be housebound, soon lose hope. Communities, at the mid-point of revitalization efforts, sink into despair due to broken promises. Vendors and funding agencies find it hard to offer grants and lines of credit to future start-ups. Volunteers and donors take less interest in similar organizations when asked to give of their time and energy. To have a nonprofit shut their doors because they failed to plan and worse, ignored the mandate God set before them, is a clear demonstration of thoughtless, reckless behavior. Whether you are engaged in ministry, the marketplace, or a combination of the two, God is calling for obedience. He is calling for faithfulness.

We have discussed both sides of the principles that impact tying the knot between faith and the marketplace. I offer one further suggestion. Not starting a nonprofit organization may be the best way to go. Perhaps becoming part of another nonprofit, that you admire and want to help, may be a better option. There are thousands of agencies, looking to expand programs and projects, in need of your expertise. You might be a perfect fit. Adding your component when fresh ideas are needed may fulfill not only your nonprofit interest, but aid in keeping their doors open. Funders and donors appreciate organizations that form collaborations with other like-minded agencies and individuals. You will still make a difference and garner much knowledge in the process. While waiting to apply the tools God makes available, tighten the knot in your own rope of experience and commitment by learning to serve.

I wrote this chapter, and everything it represents, as a stewardship guide purposed for those who love the Lord and his people.

Reinforcing the Knot ⸺∞⸺
- When a nonprofit is not adequately prepared, it walks a tightrope that hangs precariously over a river of quicksand.
- Every business succeeds or fails based on how stakeholders assume and exhibit their commitment.
- God will bless our efforts when we do the work in His name.

HURT TO WHOLENESS

Katherine LaVerne Brown

HURT TO WHOLENESS

KATHERINE LaVERNE BROWN

Is it possible to move from a place of hurt and pain to a place of wholeness in Christ? I give a resounding, "Yes!" Believe it. If you are in this place or stage in your life, be encouraged, you can make it. You can survive.

This little writing covers a span of several years—I can assure you, there is victory in Jesus Christ. I can truly say that I am blessed for this is my testimony. In the midst of a world that tends to be performance oriented, I learned to start looking within myself for validation instead of my ministry or career. The God in me sustained and brought me through.

Throughout those days of pain, hurt and humiliation, the following scripture kept coming to me. Little did I know how much I was loved by the One who loved so much. God declares in his Word, "I have loved you with an everlasting love; I have drawn you with unfailing kindness ..." (Jeremiah 31:3 NIV). But, one day I finally focused on what the Lord was saying and began to believe I was truly loved.

Are you looking for rest, peace, and tranquility? Start looking within yourself. Superb as your ministry or career may be, it is God, who loves you more than life itself, who will show you your true self-worth. Yes, even in this performance-oriented world, I have learned that God loves you and me unwaveringly.

About this Author

Katherine LaVerne Brown

Since 1993, Katherine LaVerne Brown has been a member of the Valley Kingdom Ministries International, Oak Forest, IL, under the leadership of its pastor, Apostle H. Daniel Wilson. She also serves on the board of Precious Stone Ministry, Chicago, IL.

As an anointed teacher and ordained Elder in the gospel of Jesus Christ, Katherine continues to serve in both prophetic and evangelistic capacities. Katherine's strong passion for God is balanced out with a much lighter side as she enjoys traveling, shopping, and lots of good food.

Anchored in her favorite scripture, Lamentations 3:22–25, Katherine has felt God's prompting that it is time for her to make a change and expand her ministry.

Connect with this author and speaker for your next event:
Website: *www.KBrownTeaches.com/*
Instagram: *http://Instagram.com/KathyB1204*
Email: *KBrownTeaches@gmail.com*

More from Katherine LaVerne Brown
   It's Time to Make a Change (complete small group study)
   You, Me, and We Can Succeed (youth activity workbook)
   More Than a Name: Understanding the Heart of Leah (forthcoming)
   The Power of the Communion (forthcoming)

Available Services
   Motivational Speaker and Teacher
   Workshop Instructor

HURT TO WHOLENESS

Katherine LaVerne Brown

"They found grace out in the desert, these people who survived the killing. Israel, out looking for a place to rest, met God out looking for them!" God told them, "I've never quit loving you and never will. Expect love, love, and more love! And so now I'll start over with you and build you up again, dear virgin Israel. You'll resume your singing, grabbing tambourines and joining the dance. You'll go back to your old work of planting vineyards on the Samaritan hillsides, And sit back and enjoy the fruit—oh, how you'll enjoy those harvests! The time's coming when watchmen will call out from the hilltops of Ephraim: 'On your feet! Let's go to Zion, go to meet our God!'"

—Jeremiah 31:3–6 MSG

Have you ever wondered, "What in the world is going on?" Have you been doing everything you knew to get ahead in your career or ministry? Have you raised your family, then looked around only to discover you were all alone? That's where I found myself. It seemed like nothing I did was good enough. Nothing was going as planned. I was fed up with hearing from my managers, "There is always room to improve," "You're just not cutting it," or "You are not a team player." How do I become a team player when the team doesn't want to play fair? "Lord," I began to scream, "Where did I fail?" The more I tried to please people, the more my very existence started to cease. I had become invisible—not only to others, but also to myself. I thought the world would be better off without me. I pondered if anyone would miss me if I just disappeared off the face of the earth. Walking around with a fake smile and deep hurt challenged me to believe nothing I did mattered. Yes, I had become invisible. No one saw that I was hurting. I was going through the motions of life in survival mode. I felt as though I was drowning, but there was no life preserver to be found anywhere. This weight of failure, fear, and defeat was dragging me down. Even though God had thrown me a life preserver in the opening scripture ("I have loved you with an everlasting love; I have drawn you with unfailing kindness."), I found myself screaming, "I don't want to talk to you, God, today." As much as I wanted to deny it, a dialogue had started. I was talking to God and he was talking to me. I didn't understand it then, but when I reviewed my journals, I realized a dialogue with the lover of my soul had been transpiring and leading me into all truth.

In the overview of this chapter, it was stated that we should look within ourselves for validation rather than external support. Before we go any further, let's define validation. It is to recognize, establish, or illustrate the worthiness or legitimacy of. Another meaning for validate is, to grant official sanction to by marking ("Validate." *Merriam-Webster.com*. Merriam-Webster, n.d. Web. 9 Mar. 2017). What makes us feel like we have value or worth? We are designed to want validation, the feeling of being significant in this world. The problem is that we try to get validation from what we think we have control over or the final say. When our belief system is threatened, our heart begins to die. Proverbs 4:23 encourages us to keep our heart with all diligence, for out of it springs the issues of life.

My heart had begun to die. Let's take a look at the situation. I was a single parent with two children. Where did I go wrong? I am desirable, am I not enough for this man? Apparently not, he moved on with no explanation or effort to reconcile. Yet, I kept the game face on for my children and tried to pretend it was a mutual agreement. There were women coming and laughing in my face saying things that can't be repeated. My so-called circle of friends were telling me what they knew, while thoughtlessly stating that I should have done this or that. "But, why God?" I tried to do what was right, but it was not good enough. My mother's advice: "Love someone as much as they love you." In other words, since he didn't love me anymore, I needed to move on.

I cried, "Lord I hurt; what about me?" I determined to do the things I had to do to sustain my children and me. I moved on, but this caused fear and doubt in my ability to maintain a stable relationship with potential suitors. Oh yes, there were many, but that constant dread was always there. "Lord I hurt; what about me?"

I turned to the Lord (so I thought) and poured my heart into ministry. But where did I go wrong? I had something to offer, but every idea was dismissed. I was told numerous times in the church, "You weren't called." "Who told you, you could operate in the gifts of the Spirit?" "You haven't been in the church long enough." And once again, failure, fear, and defeat were weighing me down. My mind was torn, maybe I wasn't called to do anything in this earth. I couldn't seem to perform to man's standards in my career, as a parent, a loving wife, and now ministry. I was looking for validation in ministry and in the workplace, in this performance-oriented world, instead of believing God. I kept God at arm's length— I couldn't let anyone else into my heart for the pain was just too much. Yet God kept wooing me with cords of love. I heard it again, "I have loved you with an everlasting love; I have drawn you with unfailing kindness."

I wondered if God saw how much I was hurting. Did he forget about me? I kept praying and eventually, my prayers changed to, "Lord, teach me the things I need to know to do what people are asking of me." I didn't understand the questions they were asking. I kept working in ministry and they were doing the same things to me the world did. But I kept praying, "Lord, they are my spiritual leaders, so where is the discernment and the abilities they possess to help me grow and mature?" As a lost, fearful sheep, where was I to go? What was I to do? I did the only thing I knew—I kept praying. Next, I began to study God's word for myself. But my life was still smothered in discouragement and shame. I couldn't understand why leaders in ministry and managers in the workforce continued to tear me down instead of building me up and providing the proper training to be effective in the Kingdom.

It didn't take long before I developed a bad attitude that turned into anger, which turned into bitterness. When I look back over my life, I was not a pleasant person. My ugly attitude was my defense mechanism to hide the failure, fear, and defeat. Yet I kept on praying and studying God's Word. Ravished with a spiritual hunger, I began to devour the Word of God like never before. The Lord was drawing me closer to him, yet I would only let him come so far into my soul. I needed healing and the prescription was to study, meditate, and rightly divide the Word to bring about a change and wholeness to my soul. I was fragmented and walking in delusion. It was not about me—it was all about G-O-D. God began to restore my soul and heal me from the inside out.

I turned to my church friends rather than my secular friends. They, too, ridiculed, talked, and turned their back on me. Friends are to encourage, correct, and lead in truth. Yet, my circle had decreased tremendously. It felt like they were all backstabbers. Didn't God see how much pain I was in? Where was *my* encouragement? Where was *my* exhortation? Yet I kept encouraging others, kept praying, and kept studying. I have journals and journals of my talks with God. Yet even though I would say, "I don't want to talk to you today, Lord. They hurt me and you won't do anything about it. I am determined to understand what these secular and spiritual leaders are saying to me. I don't get it Lord." Then in that small, still voice I heard it again, "I have loved you with an everlasting love; I have drawn you with unfailing kindness."

I had many things written in my journals, but all too often, I wrote the same lines:

Lord, I hurt, what about me?

I come to you daily.

I pray for the sick, now I am sick.

What about me?

What about me!

Many might know how sick I was over these past years. Yes, there were times, I couldn't walk, talk, or even breathe. I continued to press my way to ministry and work in this performance-oriented world. I did ministry when no one else came. I stood in subzero weather, prayed for church leaders, gang leaders, the homeless, the less fortunate, and wayward children. I was at the church building when it opened and when it closed. I can remember not being able to walk up the stairs when my loving son would drop me off at the elevated train station to go to a job, that didn't want me. I cried as I walked up those steps. There were occasions that I worked late hours, weekends, and holidays—and this same loving son would pick me up. Yet, I yelled at him constantly about what he didn't do. He would just look at me. I was doing to him what the world had done to me. Discouragement leads to failure, fear and defeat. Yet the Lord kept reminding me, "I have loved you with an everlasting love; I have drawn you with unfailing kindness."

One day, this loving son ran away from home. He was running to get away from a mother who only knew to spew hurt because she had been hurt. It was two, long years before my loving son would speak to me again. It was during that time, I realized I had been looking for affirmation from man instead of from the God that lived within me. And once again, God reminded me, "I have loved you with an everlasting love; I have drawn you with unfailing kindness." I finally got it. I determined to let God love me and let him teach me how to love.

We must realize there is a place of victory deep inside each one of us. The Lord is beckoning us to come in and stop standing on the threshold. He is knocking at our heart—let him in. I heard the Lord speaking to my spirit, "Let me in." Christ brings peace; just let him in. He brings restoration, revelation, exhortation, communication, a place of visitation, a place of consecration in the Lord's dwelling place of your heart.

I was about to reach my destination on my journey from hurt to wholeness. While at church one day, the Lord laid it on my heart to go to the prayer room (which was on the second floor). My heart was so heavy, I felt like I couldn't, but I went, slowly. Intercessors were already praying in the room.

When I walked in, the Lord said, "This is the last time you will deal with this sickness." I was healed from that physical ailment on the spot. I screamed. I hollered. I shouted praise to my God for being set free. My Lord didn't stop there. The next manifestation of a healing was not physical, but inner healing. My fragmented soul was healed. I felt a release in my spirit and started screaming and shouting that the Lord loved me for me. I knew I didn't have to be performance-oriented to please him. I couldn't say, "Glory, hallelujah!" loud enough. He loved me just because.

Just have faith and trust that the Lord is concerned about every little thing that pertains to us (Psalm 37:23 NLT). You see, all that praying and reading the Word of God had gotten deep in my soul and connected with my mindset. I began to believe what was written on the pages of the Bible.

So, I ask you, have you believed that you have received the Spirit of the Lord and the power of the Holy Spirit since you have been engrafted into the household of faith? If not let me help you. There is beauty in my brokenness; I truly found love, joy, and peace. The following scripture speaks on the reason why Jesus was sent. "And provide for those who grieve in Zion—to bestow on them a crown of beauty instead of ashes, the oil of joy instead of mourning, and a garment of praise instead of a spirit of despair. They will be called oaks of righteousness, a planting of the Lord for the display of his splendor" (Isaiah 61:3 NIV).

Being performance-oriented in the world means, we do everything to please man. I had neglected jumping into the glory and the presence of the Lord. I prayed, but would not come all the way into the presence. Truly, there is fullness of joy in the throne room. How did I move from hurt to wholeness? The answer was before me all time, prayer and meditation on God's Word which leads to sweet communion. Communion leads to consecration, and consecration leads to wholeness.

I would be remiss if I did not share that it was a hard and difficult road to wholeness. The more I tried, the worse it got, so I thought. "Lord, I hurt," became my silent song. I had been used and talked about. I felt my pay raises were kept to the bare minimum. I worked hard and prayed hard. Then one day I heard the Lord say, it is not about how much money you get, it is what you do with it.

Managers and co-workers challenged what I did all day. I was questioned as to why I wasn't more effective. No, I am not saying that some of the things they said were not valid, but to get this both at work and ministry was unbearable.

Christ instructed us to encourage one another as well as to teach, train and activate individuals into their destiny. Yet all I encountered was opposition. Twenty years later, I learned that the only person I needed to please was God. He taught me to study his Word to show myself approved while rightly dividing the word of truth. And yes, I learned to pray and pray some more. But that's not all I learned. God revealed to me much more. Following are some key lessons I gained from this experience that you can apply to your own life right now.

Meditate on the Word of God—make this a daily habit.

Stop limiting God—give him full access to every area of your life. Let the Holy Spirit minister the way he wants.

Journal from your heart—your time with God is so precious. Don't risk forgetting even one of those marvelous moments. Write them down. Psalms is such a wonderful example of peeking inside the hearts of men who truly loved God. Because they wrote it down, we get to benefit from their conversations with God. We see their pains, frustrations, joys, and praise. We journey through each emotion with them and come out on the other side better.

The choice is ours—it is up to each person to accept God's offer of salvation. The decision is ours. We can receive his gift of rest, peace, restoration, and life abundant or we can keep doing our own thing and continue to pay dearly.

You can move from hurt to wholeness—look for validation from inside yourself. Reach deep inside where the Father, Son, and Holy Spirit dwell.

Set goals for yourself—be careful not to overwhelm yourself. Take baby steps at first. Take one day at a time. Whatever you are facing, recognize that you can win. You must win this fight and go from hurt to wholeness.

Reinforcing the Knot —∞—
- God made you in his image and delights in you. Genesis 1:27, Zephaniah 3:17.

- He loves you with an everlasting Love. Jeremiah 31:3, John 3:16.
- His plans and thoughts toward you to fulfill your destiny and purpose are good. Jeremiah 29:11.

I Have a Purpose

Sherry Self

I Have a Purpose

Sherry Self

For everything that is created, there is a purpose. We exist to bring glory to God with our unique roles in the earth. Understanding our purpose brings our existence to life. Finding your purpose is a matter of asking, seeking, and knocking. Following these three steps will have you living on purpose every day.

ABOUT THIS AUTHOR

SHERRY SELF

As the host and executive director of her own TV show (*The Sherry Self Show*), Sherry Self has earned the reputation of being extraordinary. Sherry's knowledge, expertise, and heart are clear as she inspires her weekly viewers to "live on purpose."

In 2004, Sherry answered the call of God to preach the gospel. As this anointed evangelist preaches, she captivates her audiences by her fiery zeal. Sherry has a passion to help others see their God-given purpose through her workshops and empowerment sessions. When Sherry prays, she doesn't use empty words. She prays with power and believes God for the answers.

Connect with this author and speaker for your next event:
Instagram: *@Sherry.Self*
Facebook: *www.Facebook.com/SherryInspireYourself/*
Email: *sherryself101@yahoo.com*

More from Sherry Self:
The Sherry Self Show (weekly TV show on Comcast 31)

Available Services
Event Hosting
Professional Beauty Consultant
Inspirational Speaking
SHAPE UP: Five Factors on How God has Made Us
    Authentic (workshop)
Inspirational T-shirts

I HAVE A PURPOSE

Sherry Self

"Ask, and it will be given to you; seek, and you will find; knock, and it will be opened to you."

—Matthew 7:7 NKJV

Step 1: Ask

In the quest to live every day of your awesome life on purpose, ask. Ask the Creator why you are here. What was his purpose in creating you? We have to remember that God started everything that exists. It's in him that we find who we are and what his will is. The simple thing to do is to go to him in prayer as you meditate on his word. The creator is the only one who knows everything about his creation. Would you take your luxury automobile to a bicycle shop when it breaks down? Wouldn't it make sense to go to someone who knows how everything was put together? We would go directly to the manufacturer for repairs and tune ups. We go to the one who built the automobile and knows how it should run, what sound it should make, and all the other functions. Yes, we would take it to the one who made the automobile and knows where every bolt, nut, and wire belongs. Just as that is true for an automobile, it is the same for our lives. We should be equally as eager to go to the creator of our lives. Long before we knew, or ever heard about God, He knew us. Irrespective of whether we were planned by our parents, God planned and prepared our life purpose. He took the time and mapped out every detail, every day, and every destination about us. He knows every inner and outer working of us. And, all this happened before we made it to the earth. He knew what we would be passionate about. Our Creator, who put everything together, has given us all the tools we need to live on purpose. His desire is for us to live the way he created us. We all have a purpose, and its greater than what our minds can ever imagine. We are made by God, for God. We can trust that when we ask, the answer will be given to us.

Step 2: Seek

We shouldn't have to go far in seeking out our God given purpose. God has given us seeds of natural abilities and talents. These seeds were planted in us, and as we grow, the seeds grow. These seeds manifest themselves as those things we are good at doing—areas where we flourish naturally. It is with these talents and abilities that we can serve God best. You could call it a natural niche. These gifts, talents, abilities—seeds—can be used toward our livelihood, but they serve a deeper meaning. It's through these abilities that we are to walk in our purpose.

I want to pose a few questions. Consider your answers carefully as they are significant in helping you to get a clear understanding about your awesome life.

- What are you good at doing?
- What skill sets have you developed or mastered?
- In what areas are you receiving the most compliments, consistently? Is it your cooking, your hairdressing, singing, fashion sense? Do you speak well? We were born with the ability to encourage others—do you?

Let's not waste any more time. Look within yourself and make a self-evaluation of who you see and the work that God has given you to do. Be determined to have a "go hard or go home" attitude about yourself. Give it everything you have. Refuse to compare yourself with others. Each of us must take sole responsibility for being our best self.

Step 3: Knock

The key to knocking is being led by God to know on which doors to knock. God will show you which opportunities to take and which doors (opportunities) to leave shut. The more you begin to walk clearly in your purpose, the more prosperous openings will make themselves available to you. Be mindful that not every door is intended for you to open. Some of those doors are decoys, while others are simply meant for someone else. Seek God first. He will guide you to the right doors. You have to be careful about your moves. It is critical that you strategize every detail.

Be connected to the right people—the type of people that propel you to be the best person you can become. Think about it, if you are the smartest person in your circle, chances are you are in the wrong circle. Proverbs 27:17 says that iron sharpens iron.

Ideal opportunities stimulate circumstances to make it possible for you to be your authentic self. If you have to push or pull to get through the doors, then it's probably not the right door for you. Walking in purpose is not a struggle. God has given you a key, but it's only for your door, not someone else's.

Get Started

Your preparation will meet your destiny. Begin taking it up a notch by digging deep and wide. Research programs and people, that share the same passion as you that are successful doing it. Invest time and money in seminars, webinars, and conferences to enhance your vision and dreams. As long as you are being authentic and enjoying your purposeful life, the Bible says in Proverbs 18, that your gifts and talents will make room for you. You will begin to be exposed to people and things you never imagined. People will take notice that you're changing lives just by being yourself. Keep asking, seeking, and knocking. Put action to your vision. It's all about being creative and not holding back from doing the things you never knew you could do. God will answer your prayers and make his will for your life clear. Yes, he will open doors for you in your purposeful life.

Reinforcing the Knot

- Do a self-assessment. What are your strengths?
- God has created us all with a purpose, but we must first ask, seek, and knock.
- Whether in ministry or in the marketplace, live your God-given life on purpose.

REMOVING THE BARRIERS

Marceline Williams

REMOVING THE BARRIERS

MARCELINE WILLIAMS

We all have barriers of one sort or another. These barriers obstruct our vision, movement, and freedom to move forward. We wonder what is on the other side of the door, but the obstacles keep us guessing and questioning, yet never actually knowing.

The goal of this chapter is not only to break the barrier, but for us to break through and journey to the other side. The other side holds our blessing. The other side of the wall holds our destiny. Along our journey to breakthrough, we may encounter some areas that are not so nice. We may discover some things about ourselves that have been reinforcing the barrier. The Holy Spirit will help guide us through to victory.

Let's break through together and then help someone else break through.

About this Author

Marceline Williams

Marceline Williams is a prophetic deliverance messenger and founder of the Prayer Garden of Memphis. As an ordained and licensed minister, she is commissioned as an Apostolic Harvest Leader to preach the gospel and pray for leaders within her assigned regions.

Marceline holds a master's in business administration from Belhaven University. She also enjoys songwriting, traveling and having adventurous fun with her four children. Marceline is indeed a yielded vessel committed to prayer.

Connect with this author and speaker for your next event:
Twitter: *MemphisPrays*
Facebook: *Marceline.Williams.1*
Email: *PrayerGardenOfMemphis@gmail.com*

Forthcoming from Marceline Williams:
   The Seven Layer Prayer
   Freedom Rings
   God Wiped the Tears
   I Am Who God Says I Am
   The Demon Inside

Available Services
   Prayer Training for Leaders
   Altar Training: Do's and Don'ts
   Inspirational Speaking
   Christian Event Management

REMOVING THE BARRIERS

Marceline Williams

But seek ye first the kingdom of God, and his righteousness; and all these things shall be added unto you.

—Matthew 6:33 KJV

The barrier is thick and mortared with layers of brick that must be torn down and broken into pieces. It's a wall designed to block you from praying effectively and victoriously. This is a common experience within every believer's walk of faith.

Perhaps you have been praying for something specific, day after day, yet nothing has happened. No breakthrough. You felt empty on the inside. In the beginning, God spoke and the power of his spoken word moved things. Maybe you were wondering why your "things" weren't being moved. Keep praying. Each prayer is chipping away at those bricks. Keep praying until you breakthrough the barrier and the pieces tumble and roll away from you.

This can sometimes be religious barriers in the hidden places of the mind. From where did these apathetic mind-tricks and impossible acts of darkness ignite? The heart. Can someone instill a statement of belief in the heart or the mind? The heart is the forerunner of how the mind operates. Religious barriers will cause you to pray selfish prayers and not kingdom prayers. You are chosen to cause the kingdom of God to manifest in the earth. Manifest this kingdom by first obeying and praying for the truth of Christ to move with signs and wonders upon the earth where you are. Yes, miracles are taking place, but are any miracles actively documented in your city, state, or country?

Caring too much about what other people think is another barrier to be broken. Did you receive inspiration from Christ to do something phenomenal that will literally prove the power of God in the earth? Yes, you did. Then be about the Lord's business and don't procrastinate. No excuses.

It's time to stop doing the same things the same way. Move up. Elevation in prayer is a growing process. There are several levels of prayer. As you reach higher levels, you will begin to see a shift, and escalation in your answered prayers. This is a difficult chapter, but it will help you see your identity. Who are you exalting? For instance, discovering that you have a heavenly right to the blessings of God, through Jesus Christ, requires you to take down some barriers. Do you sometimes feel you deserve the low end? Do you feel as though it's your lot in life to always be without instead of thriving and flourishing? That barrier is a pure lie from Satan. Don't fall into the trap of negativity. Be honest and accept the boldness to change your thinking.

Realize that God wants his people to be completely dependent upon his direction. In every area of our lives, trust God—follow his leading. We consult with God for many things in our businesses. Who should our business partners be? There's another partnership that's even more crucial— our marriage partner. There is a point that must be made about marriage. Some have made wrong choices and some have made great choices. However, if there is any doubt in one's spirit about a potential spouse before marriage, then the Holy Spirit may be tugging at your heart to reveal evidence of failure later.

Emotions and the mind are revelatory of affections of the heart. Affections are the last attribute to consider when praying. The will of God (the Word of God) must be the focus. Breaking down barriers of darkness will only fall with the authority of the Word spoken—the Bible. As you pray, it must be understood that what is prayed is truth—not selfishness. Our prayers are to be to the glory and honor of God. Ask yourself this question, "Do my prayers bring glory to God or to me?" "Thy kingdom come, thy will be done on earth as it is in heaven," should be our mindset.

This statement has been shared many times; "Lord, bless me with a better job." What is the reason for a better job? Is it to buy a new home or a new car? Are you trying to improve the quality of life for your family? All of these things could be worthwhile requests.

Let's examine the following scenario about a fictitious woman we'll call, Betty. Betty prayed every day and every night. She never had enough money to pay tithes so she decided to not even try. Betty lacked the faith in God to pay her titles first and challenge God to see the outcome. However, she decided to pray 10% of her time every day. She calculated 24 hours in a day and determined she owed God two hours, forty minutes each day. She prayed one hour, twenty minutes in the morning and the same in the evening. Yet, the finances for Betty were not changing. Her mortgage continued to be late and her car note was still two months behind. Basic things like groceries and gas were often unobtainable luxuries. After this went on for about two years, Betty began to cry in her evening prayer (this had never happened before). Initially, she was praying out of routine with no intent of her heart changing towards God. As she cried and prayed, she said, "God why am I not prospering? It seems like I'm stuck?" As she was crying, her words were silenced. And now, the God she thought she knew, could speak and show Betty her error in prayer. The barrier must be removed. Yes, her prayer had become a daily routine with no true witness of communication. How was Betty to move from this place of undeveloped growth to prosperity?

Once God had Betty's attention, he showed her the process for her prayers to be heard. Betty needed to ask forgiveness from God and forgive herself for all the selfish prayers she prayed. She needed to be forgiven for not listening to the Father to speak concerning her situation. Betty changed the way she was praying by first acknowledging God as her father and praying the will of the Father. She needed to embrace Jesus not only as her Savior, but as Lord of her life. There would no longer be any decisions she would make without asking for his guidance. Once Betty made those changes, within six months, she had changed jobs with an increase in pay and caught up on her mortgage and car note.

Does it take six months for an authentic change through prayer? Not necessarily. However, it may take six months for the flesh to change and line up with God's order. Betty forgot about the things she was desiring and held to the things God desired for her. She became a tither and had more than enough left over to get the things she wanted. This illustration is a clear demonstration of Matthew 6:33–34.

Prayer is the most important element in our Christian walk. It changes us and what's around us. Don't fall for the myth that if you keep praying something must happen. That's another block to keep you praying wrong. If you keep praying selfish prayers, nothing will happen according the planned destiny of God for you. God purposely sent Moses to Mount Sinai to pray. God deliberately sent Jesus to pray. Jesus prayed (as the Scripture says in Luke 22:44) until his sweat was like blood pouring from him. There is individual prayer and corporate prayer (or group prayer). The mind must be clear and the heart turned from wickedness to genuinely approach the throne of God. Pray for God to speak to your heart. Adorn yourself for individual prayer.

There is a sweet fragrance in God's presence. Always begin prayer with praise and worship. The Bible says in Psalm 100, to make a joyful noise to the Lord. We should enter his gates with thanksgiving and into his courts with praise. Whenever we pray, we are to pray God's will. You will soon see the barriers, both hidden and exposed, be removed (1 John 5:14–15 KJV).

Reinforcing the Knot
- It's not about where you work, but it is all about where God has assigned you. He may choose to move you or keep you right where you are. Make no decisions until you've heard from him.
- God requires authentic prayer.
- Begin your prayer with praise.

THE WORD APPLIES TO ME TOO

Avis Margarete Nichols

THE WORD APPLIES TO ME TOO

AVIS MARGARETE NICHOLS

This chapter, this dialog, this process of understanding the connection between ministry and marketplace, is not just for you, it's for me too. In the process of the Holy Spirit working with me and through me to bring clarity and understanding on the divine connection of ministry and the marketplace, I am inviting you to journey with me. Together we will discover how to take what we believe and speak to others as truth for their lives relative to ministry and the marketplace, and then apply those words to our own lives.

ABOUT THIS AUTHOR

AVIS MARGARETE NICHOLS

Of all the addictions in the world, Avis Margarete Nichols has one of the best: laughing. As a mother of two, grandmother of four, and great grandmother of one, Avis has ample opportunities to indulge in her favorite pastime of laughter.

This woman of God has been visible in her community in various capacities such as a board member of multiple organizations, an event coordinator, community liaison and recruiter. She has served in areas such as adoption and foster parenting, fatherhood issues, and children's services, just to name a few.

Avis holds a bachelor's in business administration, but her love for God and his Word has inspired this evangelist to return to school in pursuit of a degree in theology.

Whether loving, laughing, or learning, Avis is forever trusting God for the next step.

Connect with this author and speaker for your next event:
Website: *www.SoaringInTheSpirit.com*
Facebook: *https://www.Facebook.com/Avis.Nichols.1*
Email: *AN@ SoaringInTheSpirit.com*

Available Services
   Motivational Speaking (*Stop Judging: You Have to
      Know Before You Can Grow*)
   Customer Service for Life Skills (secular or faith-based)
   Event Speaking for Worship, Workshops, Seminars, and
      Conferences

THE WORD APPLIES TO ME TOO

Avis Margarete Nichols

"For I know the plans I have for you," declares the Lord, "plans to prosper you and not to harm you, plans to give you hope and a future."

—Jeremiah 29:11 NIV

I have struggled with this for years. I have sold cosmetics, housewares, insurance, health plans, and the list can go on. Every time I started these ventures, I was confident in my ability to be successful. I was always the excited one on the call or the joyful one at the meeting. The people over me were also confident that I would be successful and move up high in the ranks. It has never happened. Not because of a lack of ability, skill, or knowledge. I had, or could attain, what I needed in those areas. I believe it never happened because they were not where I was supposed to be successful.

Part of the challenge in getting this right was getting to know who I was. I needed to know my life passion. Everyone has his or her own God-given passion and skillset. The question is not whether or not you can do business. The question is whether you are supposed to be doing *that* business. There would always seem to be a line that I could not cross toward the next level. It would drive me, and the people working with me, crazy. I could not reconcile if what I was doing was what God wanted me to be doing. Don't get me wrong. I'm not saying that ministry and marketplace don't come together for others in the businesses I've mentioned, I'm saying it didn't come together for me. Not because I was lazy, not because I wasn't committed, not because I lacked anything, it just wasn't for me. In ministry, we believe there is a call of service on our lives and we have to strive to align what we are doing with that call. If we do not, the result could be disastrous for us and others. Being in compliance with God in the call of service he has placed on our life is the ministry part. Finding out how it aligns with the business we are in, or launching, is the marketplace. Having peace with God, as we are making money, should be the driving goal of determining success. But, we cannot accomplish that if we do not know the plan God has for our lives.

As we examine three points from this chapter's main verse, the goal is to move toward understanding that even though we help others by encouraging, supporting and assisting them in attaining their goals, this is a personal journey also. Indeed the Word applies to me too.

'Believe' is our first point, followed by 'trust,' and then 'the benefit of obedience.'

Believe: "For I know the plans I have for you."

The word *believe* is not a big word in size. However, by way of definition, it has been, and continues to be, a word that serves as the basis for songs, movies, plays, conversations, disagreements, self-esteem, pride, confusion, joy, sorrow, and more. By definition, *believe* means: (1) an acceptance that a statement is true or that something exists. (2) trust, faith, or confidence in someone or something ("Belief." *Merriam-Webster.com*. Merriam-Webster, n.d. Web. 9 Mar. 2017). Hence, what we believe becomes a foundational basis for how we will walk, talk and live our lives internally and externally.

In a letter Jeremiah the prophet is having delivered to the exiles of Jerusalem to Babylon, he lets the people know that the words he has pinned to them are not his words but words from the Lord Almighty, the God of Israel. God lets the exiles know that he, the Lord, has plans for them.

Just as God had plans for them, he has plans for us, but we have to believe. We have to accept it to be true. When we don't believe, we struggle. When we don't believe, we can become stubborn, abusive, ungrateful, and uncaring. When we don't believe, we don't see the relevance or the connection in doing what we're doing. It's futile to us. Sometimes it's not that we don't believe in God, it's that we don't believe in ourselves. Do you see the irony here that Jeremiah would be the messenger of this word to the exiles? Jeremiah was the one who said to God, after he had been called to go forth as a prophet, "Then said I, Ah, Lord God! behold, I cannot speak: for I am a child" (Jeremiah 1:6 KJV). Essentially, God's response was to tell Jeremiah not to say that to him. God told Jeremiah that he was to go where he sent him and say what he told him to say. Because he is such a loving God, he also told him not to be afraid because he would with him. He told him he would deliver him.

In order for Jeremiah to have written the chapter and verses we are reviewing today, Jeremiah had to believe in what God was telling him and have faith that it would come to pass. The Word spoken to Jeremiah applies to me too. I have to believe those words and step out in faith. I have to believe that the marketplace business I'm in, is in the will of God—even if no one else can see it and even if I'm in the midst of struggle.

Trust: "... plans to prosper you and not to harm you,..."

Whether we take the prosper aspect of the verse literally or figuratively, they had to trust that God's process was for their good and not intended to bring them harm. In the letter, God told the exiles to live where they were planted at that moment. Don't stop building, marrying, having children; live. What you are going through right now is all a part of a greater plan. What we may not see right now is that God is going to deliver us and restore (prosper) us. We must learn to trust God that he will do what he says.

When we view the word 'prosper' from a figurative point as in denoting prosperity, it doesn't subtract from the truth that we are to trust God in the process. In our early days, our money may not line up the way we expect, but God, when we are in his will, will straighten that out in the process. Perhaps we may have to take some business training. We may have to learn some business lessons through life that no book can teach us. We may have to suffer with self and learn to let go of some stuff, some things, and some people that may be hindering our progress. God's plans require us to trust him. I can quote Proverbs 3: 5–6 KJV, "Trust in the LORD with all thine heart; and lean not unto thine own understanding. In all thy ways acknowledge him, and he shall direct thy paths," to someone else all day long and believe it for them because it's true. But the application of that truth to my personal life in the midst of my trials, struggles, disappointments, doubts, fears, disillusionment, discouragement, and failures is the challenge. It's personal! Yes, the Word applies to me too.

The Benefit of Obedience: "... plans to give you a hope and a future."

We have to believe and trust that what we are going through is for a purpose. It doesn't end here. The exiles had to believe that God was talking to them through Jeremiah. They had to trust that as they went about the business of living in their 'right now' and doing their best in obedience to the instructions they'd been given; there would be a brighter day ahead. God promised them hope and a future, and God does not renege on his promises. For the purpose of this book's subject, I'm not going to go into the spiritual connotations of what this is saying to me, but I could. I could very easily go into the promise of hope being in Christ and our future being eternal life, reigning with him in glory. I could, but I won't.

The benefit of obedience is the fulfillment of God's promises. We cannot challenge God, regarding his promises, when things aren't working or going the way we envisioned it. Let's be careful to check ourselves before we wreck ourselves. A large part of being successful in ministry and the marketplace is obedience. We are called to obey the will, the way, and the plans of God. Always remember, we don't belong to ourselves nor do our businesses belong to us. We may have the birth certificates and the titles but everything belongs to God.

As we obey and seek first the kingdom of God, we should believe and trust that all the other things will be added at the proper time, in the proper way and in the proper season.

THE WORD APPLIES TO ME TOO!

We look together at the sky and I say,
there is no limit for you.
We study the Word together and I say there is no secret
what God can do; for you.
I preach and I teach the principle
all things are possible with God; for you.
So, I push and I prod. I encourage and commend.
I support, I suggest, I listen and I defend.
I won't let you stop, I won't let you quit.
I believe and I see that this dream
can come to pass; for you.
But, what I keep overlooking in this process
Is that the same Word applies to me too.

Reinforcing the Knot

- Whether in the marketplace or my ministry, the Word applies to you and to me.
- We must believe in God. We must trust God.
- We must be obedient to God.

WOMEN, WORK, AND WEALTH

Tanya E. Lawrence

WOMEN, WORK, AND WEALTH

TANYA E. LAWRENCE

The option to work outside the home is a luxury few can afford. Some of us work because we want to utilize our gifts and talents in a much bigger way. Yet for the vast majority of us, we've gotten accustomed to eating regular meals and having a roof over our heads—so we must work.

We work, we work, we work, we do family, and we work some more. We end the day with little to show for our efforts. Our families are strained, the income is meager, and the frustrations are high. And, what happened to the ministry?

The next few pages are some things I learned along the way on my journey to balancing family, life, work, and ministry.

ABOUT THIS AUTHOR

TANYA E. LAWRENCE

Tanya Lawrence is truly a multifaceted author. Her fun side loves sweet tea, gummy bears, and traveling to exotic places. As the holder of both a bachelor's and a master's degree in business management, along with an additional master's degree in management information systems, it's clear that Tanya is also well educated. Currently, she serves as an executive assistant for a large corporation.

Most importantly, Tanya has a passion for her Savior, Jesus Christ. She demonstrates this in her faithfulness to her church as she serves on the praise team as well as serving as the secretary/treasurer for her church's district. However, nothing keeps her as grounded as when she's teaching the two to six-year-olds in Sunday school. Tanya's unique personality keeps her fan base ever growing.

Connect with this author and speaker for your next event:
Facebook: *http://Facebook.com/TanyaLawrence/*
Email: *cottonpatchpg@gmail.com*

More from Tanya E. Lawrence:
   Priceless (a ministry, in development, devoted to helping others see their true worth in Christ)

Available Services
   Travel Consultant (CPPG Travel–owner)
   Property Management Service (CottonPatch Property Group, LLC–owner)

WOMEN, WORK, AND WEALTH

Tanya E. Lawrence

Let your light so shine before men, that they may see your good works, and glorify your Father which is in heaven.

—Matthew 5:16 KJV

Women in the Workplace

Throughout the portals of time, a woman's place in society has had a myriad of challenges. In a world dominated by men in prestigious positions of power, a woman in the workforce has often been viewed as insignificant or minimal. However, due to ever changing socio-economic issues and cultural evolution, women have been making a broader stance and have a more acclimated presence in the marketplace.

As a young girl going through school, I watched my mother work two jobs trying to provide for our family. I saw how tired she would often be. I saw that she never had much time for herself nor some of the simplest pleasures of life. My father also worked, but was often out of town because the market in which he had his trade was more profitable in a different city from where we resided. I often found myself missing them because their jobs consumed them. This made me begin to think about my own future. How could I balance both work and family life?

When I became an adult, I began a career in corporate America—where many women were making great strides and their voices were being heard. They were now able to stand in key positions, such as managers, executives, and

131

even CEOs of companies. I felt proud as a woman to see other women breaking the barriers and becoming more liberated to make their mark in the marketplace—the place where men used to dominate. I remember looking at myself in the mirror one day and thinking, "You are a woman, you can do it, too!" I love helping people, and what better movement than to help other people, especially women in the marketplace.

Work Until You Win

After 20 years of working in the corporate field and being a single mother of three very active children, I found myself falling in the same scenario as my parents. I was working continuously. There was no balance to achieve the time and financial freedom I sought initially. My children suffered. I suffered.

Working as a dedicated employee is what many of us start out striving to do. For most, this is Plan A. What happens when Plan A doesn't yield the results that you had often longed for? For me I had reached a pinnacle in my corporate career. I realized what I was seeking had to now become my Plan B. I began to ask God, "How can I create the lifestyle that I desire, while still being able to balance my life with work, church, and a family?" It was then, my mindset had to make a shift to go from employee to entrepreneur.

Throughout the duration of my corporate career, I've met numerous great and influential people. I've gained a wealth of knowledge and skills, all of which came with purpose. This purpose led to the plan God had predestined for me all along. My life has been transformed from *process* to *purpose*. My tenure in the corporate culture helped position me for my purpose in ministry.

Oftentimes while I worked as an employee, I would have days when I would be discouraged, distressed, and many times, disappointed, but I learned to create synergy in my mind by looking for the small victories in every day. Instead of focusing on my obstacles and adversities, I had to create balance and look at everything as a teachable moment.

As I continued to seek the Lord for direction and an understanding of my passion for helping others, especially women, questions began to surface. I needed God to show me how I could help empower other women, how I could teach them the possibilities of equality, while exemplifying his love and grace throughout everything I did. How was I going to step into a new realm in the marketplace? I needed to know how I could supplement my corporate income in order to be able to use my gifts and natural talents while still having time and financial freedom. I had the questions, but I knew God was the source of all my answers.

Hearing God's Voice

The answer did not come right away; however, the vision had been planted in me a long time ago. I remember taking a part-time seasonal job, knowing I did not want to work two jobs long term, as I saw my mother do for many years. In this short time, God showed me a vision. I did not know how it would all come to pass and quite frankly, I was not even sure it would ever come to pass. I've heard it said and I believe it that when God gives a vision, he will make provision, especially as we continue to trust him and seek his will for our lives. Although, it took approximately 15 years for it to all come together, I stand as a proud owner of multiple businesses. I am grateful that the day I heard him speak to my heart and show me the vision, I remained steadfast and did not lose sight of what he showed me.

To the women who face many, less-than-ideal situations, and you're wondering what in the world is going on, it's called, "life." Obstacles may come, hurdles will be there, relationships will fail, times may get hard, but these are just mere growing pains that will make you strong if you are determined to win.

Work Towards Wealth

Women have a natural inclination to be nurturing and task orientated. A strong-minded and virtuous woman will work endlessly to obtain her goals. She understands that her reward is far greater than just completing the task at hand. The Bible asks the question, "Who can find a virtuous woman?" and goes on to state her value as being far above rubies (Proverbs 31:10 KJV).

I believe, that as women, once we realize how to create vision, set our goals, and continue to work until we win, the wealth will come. In persistence, we will gain a wealth of knowledge, a wealth of resources, a wealth of opportunities, a wealth of teachable moments, and ultimately wealth in our time and finances.

Reflecting on my transition from employee to entrepreneur, I initially thought my pursuit of wealth was primarily to gain financially. I believed, "... money answereth all things" (Ecclesiastes 10:19 KJV). I later realized that, yes, money could make things easier, but true wealth was far more important than money.

When I started my first business, I began to see that my past experiences were necessary in grooming me for future endeavors. That knowledge allowed me to minister in a new way. God created other avenues for me to minister to others. I expanded my business into the network marketing industry and I found that it brought me much more joy and gratification to see others achieve the goals they were seeking. For me, wealth became defined as being able to help others alongside yourself. Zig Ziglar said it best, "You can have everything in life you want, if you will just help other people get what they want." I found this to be so true. It has helped shape how I look at business.

I no longer looked at business as usual, but rather looked at it as ministry. Some people think that ministry is just standing in a pulpit preaching the gospel or compelling a large congregation; however, ministry is so much more than that. It's about touching people's lives where they are and providing a resource to help them achieve more in their life. I am happy and grateful that God has blessed me to have many talents and gifts, but he has also allowed me to be a gift.

As women in the marketplace we often carry a lot on our shoulders and sometimes we may feel that we are not deserving of our equitable place on the corporate ladders of the world. But, I am here to encourage you, that you can achieve anything that you put your mind, focus, and energy into. Women, as you go about your journey in life and seek your purpose remember, "In all thy ways acknowledge him, and he shall direct thy paths" (Proverbs 3:6 KJV).

Reinforcing the Knot

- Know that if God gives you a vision, he will provide provision. Always keep God first.
- As life's adversities come, keep working until you win. Look for the victories in each day.

- Don't be afraid of who God called you to be. Most importantly, share your wealth, for it is part of your ministry.

FEAR DOESN'T LIVE HERE ANYMORE: KICK FEAR TO THE CURB AND FINALLY START YOUR BUSINESS

Beverly Walthour

Fear Doesn't Live Here Anymore: Kick Fear to the Curb and Finally Start Your Business

Beverly Walthour

Fear comes in many forms: fear of failure, fear of not being good enough, fear of the unknown, and fear of success. In this chapter, you will learn five daily strategies, that you can incorporate immediately, to help you overcome these fears and finally get your business started.

ABOUT THIS AUTHOR

BEVERLY WALTHOUR

As a former middle school math instructor, Beverly Walthour has learned to trust God every day for wisdom. Indeed prayer became her daily sustenance.

Although still relying on God, Beverly is now a business strategist for professional women, in their thirties, who work full-time and want to start an online business. Beverly's passion to see others succeed shines as she empowers women with tips, strategies, resources, and the much needed support to plan, launch, and grow their own businesses.

Beverly loves helping others, but she also knows that she has to take time out for herself. In her spare time, she loves to read, bowl, and lie on the beach. When she really wants to take some "me time," she enjoys her favorite chocolate cookie bar treats by eating all the chocolate off first, then digging into the crunchy cookie. Beverly treasures her work and her playtime.

Connect with this author and speaker for your next event:
Website: *http://BeverlyWalthour.com/*
Facebook: *www.Facebook.com/CoachBeverlyWalthour*
Email: *Beverly@BeverlyWalthour.com*

Available Services
    Business Strategist
    Private and Group Coaching
    Inspirational Speaking: (topics)
        How to Start Your Online Business
        How to Eliminate Fear and Start Your Business
        How to Use Social Media to Grow Your Online
            Business

FEAR DOESN'T LIVE HERE ANYMORE: KICK FEAR TO THE CURB AND FINALLY START YOUR BUSINESS

Beverly Walthour

For God has not given us a spirit of fear, but of power and of love and of a sound mind.

—2 Timothy 1:7 NKJV

If you have ever thought about starting an online business, or brick and mortar, but haven't—keep reading. This chapter is for you. As a business strategist, I educate women, who work full-time and want to start a business, on how to successfully get their business up and running.

The first question I ask is: "What's stopping you from starting your own business?" Whenever I ask this question, I expect to hear that the lack of funds is the top reason. However, 98% of the time, I get a completely different response. The overwhelming reason I'm given is actually a fairly small word with a massive impact. F-E-A-R. Yes, fear.

Most often, the responses are something along the lines of:

- What if I fail and have to go back to my 9-5? (Fear of failure)
- What if my business takes off faster than I can keep up with it? (Fear of success)
- What if I can't balance working full-time, my family, and starting a new business? (Fear of the unknown)
- What if my family and friends don't support my new business? (Fear of not being supported)

- What if I can't make a consistent income? What about benefits and a retirement fund? (Fear of the unknown)

Fear, fear, and more fear. All of these questions were wrapped in fear. Even worse, many people did not realize fear as the culprit. Have you found yourself stuck in a "What if?" question? Have any of these fears kept you locked in a job in which you were not happy? Have any of these fears kept you from pursuing a business you know in your heart was meant for you to start? If you answered, "Yes" to any of these questions, you are not alone. Unfortunately, for many people, fear has kept them from fulfilling their ultimate dream of becoming an entrepreneur.

As I continue working with these women, the next question I ask is, "What is your 'why' for wanting to start your business?" The responses usually focus around the following:

- They want to be able to control their schedules. They're tired of missing their children's events or scrabbling to rearrange work schedules so that they can attend.
- They want the financial freedom to pay off debt and live the lifestyle they've always dreamed about. They want to be able to purchase things without looking at the price tag, have money in their savings account, and enough money to live comfortably once they retire.
- They want to have a business in which they get to help other people live a better life.

Do any of these rationales sound familiar to you? Is there something else that you would add? As I talk to these women, I see myself in each and every one of them. My "why" for being a business strategist is similar to theirs. As I listen to their stories, my eyes fill with tears, because I remember what it was like working a job in which I was miserable going to everyday. I remember tears popping in my eyes when the alarm would go off each weekday morning. I remember every Monday wishing it was Friday.

On the flip side, I knew what it was like to have a career I loved, but I felt that something was missing. I questioned myself, "Shouldn't I be happy to have a job I love?" There are people who would kill to have that. However, I knew God did not intend for me to live in a constant state of confusion and doubt. I knew there was something more for me. I just had to figure out what it was.

Part of My Journey.

I received my undergraduate degree in middle school education and I began my career as a middle school math teacher in 2000. By 2007, I was ready to leave the classroom. I no longer felt happy when I went to work. I felt I had done everything I could in that position. Additionally, I had gotten a master's degree and held various teacher leadership positions. Since my district was small, chances for upward movement were very slim.

Around that time, a friend of mine, who was also a teacher, had started her own tutoring company successfully. She told me that she had replaced her teacher salary and that I should start a tutoring company too. I stepped out in faith, resigned from my teaching position, and starting a tutoring company of my own.

Although I had the skill set, since I was an educator, I had not prepared myself for the business aspect of being an entrepreneur. Furthermore, I had not prepared myself mentally to be an entrepreneur. Although I was able to generate clients and some profit, I was not able to do so consistently. That's when fear and doubt started to creep in. I started asking a lot of "What if?" questions. "What if I can't do this consistently?" "What if I get sick, how will I make money?" "What if I don't maintain enough clients to keep up with my current lifestyle?" What if, What if, What if? Then those "What if's" started sounding like, "Well, if you go back to the classroom, you know exactly what to expect." Although I felt some people would think I was a failure, two years after starting my business, I decided to close it and go back into the classroom.

At least as a classroom teacher, I knew I would get a consistent paycheck, health benefits, the summers off, but most importantly, I would have job security. For seven years, I was back in the classroom, where I had the safety and security I felt I needed. However, there was always this thing nagging in the back of my mind. I always questioned if I had given up too soon. I wondered what was the reason God had me go through this process. What was I supposed to have learned?

The answer to that question was not understood fully until recently. Fast-forward ten years, I had left the classroom to pursue what I absolutely love doing—I was now a trainer. However, that desire to be an entrepreneur never went away. I successfully started two more home-based businesses, but I kept thinking back to my first business; what could I have done differently? Now, I can truly say I learned a lot from that experience. I would not trade it for anything. Why do I say that? I say it because it has enabled me to become a stronger strategist and entrepreneur.

I can completely relate to my clients who struggle with the fear of starting and maintaining a business, because I have been there. When I tell women that I understand how fear can keep them in a situation or move them out of a situation, I know first-hand. I know the kind of fear that keeps them in a job they are no longer happy doing. I know the kind of fear that scares them when they experience success. I know the kind of fear that makes them stay in a situation either because they don't want to let other people down or they don't want to hear them say "I told you so." When I begin to experience that fear, I go back to my scripture: God has not given us a spirit of fear but of power and of love and a sound mind (2 Timothy 1:7 NKJV).

Since I know God did not give us a spirit of fear, as a business strategist, one of the first things I address with the women I work with is that fear. I help them incorporate strategies that are designed to help them kick fear to the curb. We develop what is called a "success mindset." These mindset strategies are essential to helping them cope when their business is not moving in the way they intended. Let's discuss the five strategies I encourage my clients to incorporate daily:

Strategy #1: Set Weekly Business Goals

At the beginning of each week, make a habit of establishing two or three business goals. These goals should be written in a journal. There is power in writing out your goals because it then holds you accountable and allows you to track your progress toward reaching them. I truly believe in making S.M.A.R.T goals; these are goals that are specific, measurable, attainable, realistic, and timely. They force us to be laser focused. I can set them weekly, monthly, quarterly, yearly, etc. Following are just a few examples of *smart* goals:

145

- I will apply for my business license by Friday, October 14.
- I will finish my website by Friday, November 11.
- I will write my exit strategy for my full-time job by Friday, November 11.

Halfway through your week, month, quarter, and/or year, do a reflection in your journal on your progress. At the end of your time, reflect on whether or not you reached the goal. If you did, celebrate. If you did not reach your goal, reflect on what happened and what you can do differently. Then go out and enjoy yourself.

Strategy #2: Visualization

Visualization involves you creating a mental account of a major milestone in your business (e.g., getting your first paying client, achieving your first 5-figure month, etc.). Write out this account in vivid detail. Include such things as what you are wearing, what you are saying, what you are doing, etc., when you experience that milestone. Play this mental picture over and over in your mind daily.

Strategy #3: Affirmations

Affirmations involve both writing and speaking positive, powerful statements about your business. A couple of examples may include: "I am a successful and profitable businesswoman." "I attract my ideal clients every day." Have about 10-15 affirmations that you speak everyday throughout your day. As a frequent reminder, post them around your home, your office, and in your car.

Strategy #4: Read

Another powerful strategy to use is to read at least ten minutes per day. Your reading should include things that can help grow your mind and your business. Furthermore, as an entrepreneur, you should always stay abreast of current trends in your industry and market. Investing in your professional development is key to the growth of your business.

Strategy #5: Journal Writing

Having a dedicated place to document your business journey is extremely helpful to your business. Use your journal to record your weekly goals, visualizations, affirmations, and daily/weekly reflections. Writing things down is an excellent way to hold yourself accountable, keep track of your accomplishments, and document your business growth.

By incorporating these five strategies, you are training your mind to focus on success instead of fear. I'm not saying that fear and doubt will not pop up, but when they do, you have five strategies you can use to kick them right back to the curb. If you are ready to start your business, I strongly encourage you to begin using these strategies immediately. You will certainly see a change in the way you think about starting your business.

Reinforcing the Knot

- Implement a daily success mindset routine. This is key to the success of your business.

- Know that God did not give us a spirit of fear. This is critical in keeping us focused on what God has created us to do.
- Use your services/products your business offers to help others overcome obstacles in their lives. You have value. People are waiting to hear your message. Remember, fear can't live here anymore. Kick it to the curb and finally get your business started.

AFTERWORD

Over the years, I've learned many lessons. The following pages contain a few nuggets of advice I would recommend to professional business women, men who serve in ministry (or business) with women, and those with start-up businesses led by women faithpreneurs. Yes, these next words are for you.

Keep the Lord first in all you do.

Surround yourself with intelligent, God-fearing people.

Model the way you want to be respected and treated.

Build strong and diversified networks.

Take responsibility for your part and accept the change.

Play well with others.

Acknowledge that nothing stays the same.

Understand that quality collaborations and partnerships are key.

Know your own strengths and weaknesses.

Use your strengths to address your weaknesses.

Value your haters. They make you greater.

Find balance in your daily life.

Be confident and competent.

Believe in yourself.

Become a master juggler.

Believe when someone shows you who they really are.

Create a professional presence (even on social media).

Choose your personal and professional circle wisely.

Self-confidence breeds success.

Do not work harder for an employer than you do for yourself.

Multiple streams of income are necessary.

Don't hold grudges; you may need to keep your enemies close.

Refocusing to a new assignment, may change your location.

Getting acquainted with new assignments require time.

Reevaluate your progress, pursuits, and potential.

Develop your endurance.

Pursue spiritual renewal and transformation.

Get paid to do what you love and are passionate about.

Have a good coach and mentor for several years of your life.

WORKING IT OUT

Use the spaces below to record how this book has spoken to your life.

_____
_____
_____
_____
_____

What are some things you have learned?

_____
_____
_____
_____
_____

What are the things you need to start doing?

_____
_____
_____
_____
_____

What are the things you need to stop doing?

_____

_____

_____

_____

_____

What are the hindrances in your life? What do you need to do about them?

_____

_____

_____

_____

_____

Right where you are, how can you begin to tie ministry to the marketplace?

_____

_____

_____

_____

_____

What's next for you? What are your action steps?

- _____

- _____

- _____

MEET DEBORA D. TAYLOR

Debora Taylor is the founder and president of Taylor-Made International Institute and the para-church ministry, the Women's Faith and Business: *Tying the Knot between Ministry and the Marketplace.* She received her formal education from the Milwaukee Theological Institute and the Spring Field College with a bachelor's in human services.

She was raised in the inner city in the West Lawn housing project. Although she was an atheist for most of her teen and young adult years, at the age of twenty-six, God touched her life. Through the supernatural power of the Holy Spirit, she made her confession for the Lord Jesus Christ. Her life was changed that day, and she has never been the same.

Debora has been a spiritual and integral leader in the human service field for more than twenty-five years with expertise in the areas of women's issues, marriage and family enrichment, youth and early childhood, and responsible fatherhood. Her efforts, her enthusiasm, and her great successes continue to be recognized locally and nationally. Debora has a long list of honors and awards including, the National Presidential Volunteer Service Award for 2012 presented to her by President Barak Obama for her local, regional and national involvement through the United States.

By the leading of the Holy Spirit, Debora and her husband became organizers and church planters of the New Life Kingdom Ministries International. She co-pastored for 18 years with her husband, Pastor Guy Taylor, until retiring from pulpit ministry in 2013 to move south to Memphis, Tennessee. She has been an ordained minister for twenty-eight years.

Debora, fondly known as "Pastor D," serves in ministry partnership with Apostle Ricky D. Floyd and Pastor Shelia

Floyd of Pursuit of God Transformation Center International in Memphis, Tennessee.

Debora Taylor, a native of Milwaukee, Wisconsin, now resides in Collierville, Tennessee with her husband. They have two adult children: Nyshi Taylor-Williams and Dominique Taylor. The loves of her life are her granddaughters: My'Asha and Gracelyn.

Debora D. Taylor—International Best-Selling Author
Co-authored projects:
> *Bruised But Not Broken*
> Compiler: Linda Ellis Eastman

> *Boys to Men: The Guide for African American Boys*
> Compiler: Linda Ellis Eastman

> *Empowered Women of Social Media Volume 1*
> Compiler: Carla Hall and Denise Thompson

> *Empowered Women of Social Media:*
>   *Finding Global Unity*
> Compiler: Carla Hall and Denise Thompson

> *Chocolate & Diamonds for the Woman's Soul*
>   *Celebrating the Majesty of Motherhood*
> Compiler: Hot Pink Publishing

Connect with Debora D. Taylor for your next event:
Website: *www.DeboraDTaylor.com*
Facebook: *Facebook.com/groups/WomensFaithandBusiness/*
Email: *DeboraDTaylor@DeboraDTaylor.com*

Taylor-Made International Institute
P.O. Box 1554
Collierville, TN 38027